Nurturing Narratives

COACHING COMPREHENSION • CREATING CONVERSATION

Nurturing Narratives

Story-based language intervention for children with language impairments
that are complicated by other developmental disabilities such as
autism spectrum disorders

Lauren Franke, Psy.D., and Christine Durbin, M.A.

Foreword by Brenda Smith Myles

© 2011 AAPC
P.O. Box 23173
Shawnee Mission, Kansas 66283-0173
www.aapcpublishing.net

Publisher's Cataloging-in-Publication

Franke, Lauren.

    Nurturing narratives : story-based language intervention for children with language impairments that are complicated by other developmental disabilities such as autism spectrum disorders / Lauren Franke and Christine Durbin ; foreword by Brenda Smith Myles. -- Shawnee Mission, Kan. : AAPC Publishing, c2011.

    p. ; cm. + CD-ROM.

    ISBN: 978-1-934575-69-7
    LCCN: 2011921276
    At head of title: Coaching comprehension, creating conversation.
    Accompanying CD-ROM contains assessment tools and worksheets.
    Includes bibliographical references and index.

    1. Autism spectrum disorders--Patients--Language. 2. Autistic children--Language. 3. Language disorders in children--Treatment. 4. Speech therapists--Handbooks, manuals, etc. 5. Teachers of children with disabilities--Handbooks, manuals, etc. I. Durbin, Christine. II. Title.

RJ506.A9 F73 2011
618.92/85882--dc22   1102

This book is designed in Helvetica Neue.

Cover art © iStockPhoto.com

Printed in the United States of America.

Dedication

I dedicate this book to my husband, whose advice, support, and patience made this book possible.

L. F.

I dedicate this book to my wonderful mother, Joan Butcher, the rest of my family, and Cloud Hands (my other family) for all of their marvelous support during the process of writing this book.

C. D.

Table of Contents

Appendices (see accompanying CD)

Appendix A: Resources for Creating Tailored Stories

Appendix B: Sample Tailored Stories with Pictures in PowerPoint

Appendix C: Informal Assessment, Sample Goals, and Record Keeping

Appendix D: Group Therapy

Appendix E: Nurturing Narratives and Story Grammar

Appendix F: Evidence-Based Support for Nurturing Narratives

Appendix G: Additional Personal Narrative Activities

Acknowledgments

The Coaching Comprehension-Creating Conversation: Nurturing Narratives (CCCC: NN) approach was developed for the children we work with who have complicated language problems. We are indebted to these children for helping us learn how to make story-centered therapy meaningful, manageable, engaging, and productive for them. We also want to thank the children's parents, who for more than 30 years have sparked our thoughts and allowed us to review video tapes, test ideas, and share their children's ups and downs during the training of others. We are extremely grateful for their enthusiasm, support, and fabulous feedback and collaboration throughout the lengthy development of CCCC: NN.

We also wish to express exceptional gratitude to the numerous past and present scholars and practitioners in our field whose collective work and wisdom have influenced our work so much. There are far too many to mention here, but we would like to acknowledge one – Dr. Judith Johnston. Her research and writing on the relationships between linguistic and cognitive development, in particular, have made a major contribution to our thoughts about children's language intervention and to the writing of this book.

In addition to the children and their families, and scholars in our field, numerous others have offered us exceedingly valuable assistance, and we would each like to acknowledge some of these exceptional people:

Lauren's Thanks:

The completion of this project relied on a tremendous amount of support from my speech pathology buddies, teachers, students, and administrators throughout the Orange County Department of Education in southern California. This book would not have happened without the initial "push" from Andrea Walker to put this "out there." As coordinator of the S.U.C.S.E.S.S. Project for the Orange County of Education, she provided me with opportunities to train hundreds of SLPs over the years and to follow up with them through an ongoing mentor group. This group continues to meet, develop ideas, and share curriculum materials. Her encouragement, feedback, and opportunities to collaborate were such an appreciated source of support and will never be forgotten. Dr. Janet Dodd, from Chapman University, was always there to bounce ideas off of. After her visits to schools supervising her graduate students, it was gratifying and exciting to hear talk about how her students were using CCCC: NN at their school sites. Dr. Dodd also graciously contributed to this manual by adding her expertise about using CCCC: NN with groups in the schools.

Finally, Dan Feshbach, a parent of a student with autism, inspired me almost since the conception of this approach. His support, enthusiasm and vision have always been and continue to be a source of inspiration.

Chris's Thanks:

I want to express deep gratitude to my wonderful SLP friends who have contributed so much to this book. Immense thanks go to Patty Toboni, Maureen McKeown, and Amanda Gean (the one responsible for the brilliant idea of "A Month of Stories"), for thoughtful reading of version after version, and for offering invaluable input throughout the process of the writing of this book. They, along with my other amazing colleagues, Tricia Evans, Molly O'Shea, and Leigh Klibowitz, have enthusiastically embraced this story-based intervention, enriched it in countless ways with their wonderfully innovative ideas, and given me tremendous support. I am grateful too to Amanda Cornelius for hours and hours of thought-provoking, problem-solving conversations about the children we see and how best to treat them. Many thanks also to Carol Freidenberg and Flo Kimmerling for generously reading, and sharing their wise ideas about, the earliest version of this book; and another special thank you to Flo for also reading the book in its final version and being so wonderfully encouraging.

Much gratitude also goes to Suzanne Giraudo, clinical director, and Karen Norman, manager, at the Kalmanowitz Child Development Center at California Pacific Medical Center, where I work, for their dedication to the children and families we serve and incredible leadership and support of our staff. Their encouragement and support of this project, and countless other projects I and other staff have been passionate about, have been terrific. They have created an outstanding center to support us in doing the work that we love.

Acknowledgments

Many thanks also go to my fabulous friends Betty Kirksey, special educator, school administrator, and autism specialist, and phenomenal poet, Nancy Hoffman, for reading the midway version of the book and offering their unique and most helpful feedback and suggestions. Thanks to Kelly Mackin for zeroing right in and giving great pointed feedback regarding some core needs in the book. And thanks too to my sister, Nancy Durbin, for her "assistance fantastique" with proofing and wording – she's a marvelous wordsmith. Last, but definitely not least, tremendous appreciation goes to Jerome Schwab for the countless times he shared his writing expertise with me, for his thoughtful and valuable suggestions, and for all his support during the writing of this book.

Finally, we both would like to thank Kirsten McBride, our editor, and the staff at AAPC for all their guidance, and for collaborating with us so closely to create this book!

Preface

We are excited to share *Coaching Comprehension-Creating Conversation: Nurturing Narratives* (CCCC: NN) with you. The story behind CCCC: NN began more than 10 years ago in southern California. Lauren was working with some children who were not engaged, motivated, or making expected progress in their language intervention. Some of the children were experiencing growing behavior problems. In response to these children's difficulties, she began developing Coaching Comprehension-Creating Conversation, a functional, motivating, and fun language intervention approach designed to address language and social communication skills that support social and academic growth.

Meanwhile, in northern California, Chris was having a repeated experience of running into stumbling blocks when she attempted to introduce stories into language therapy for children who demonstrated more significant language difficulties. As these children would progress to using simple sentence patterns, she often thought it might be time to move beyond single sentences into the broader context of simple stories. She would start with a simple two- or three-picture sequence story but, more often than not, the activity flopped. Often, the children did not seem to grasp that the pictures were related or that the pictures and text were part of one connected story.

Chris looked into various narrative therapy approaches, but the ones she found were geared for much higher functioning children. Then she learned about the narrative intervention component that Lauren had incorporated into her Coaching Comprehension-Creating Conversation model. She was pleased with the results she experienced and excited about the potential of narrative-based intervention for lower functioning children. Approximately five years ago, Lauren and Chris teamed up to further develop the model, and write this book.

Nurturing Narratives is a story-based language intervention approach that embeds building language skills into the context of sharing personal narratives and retelling fictional stories. It was developed for children with language impairments that are complicated by other developmental issues such as autism and/or intellectual disabilities. Often, a common characteristic shared by these children is a severe receptive language deficit. We agree with Twachtman-Cullen (1997), who says that "comprehension [is] … the power that fuels expression" (p. 9), and believe that using a language intervention framework that emphasizes comprehension is critical for facilitating expressive language development.

The Nurturing Narratives model is comprised of two major components, Tailored Stories and the 4 M's. Tailored Stories contain simplified and/or reformulated story content that matches the child's levels of linguistic and cognitive processing to ensure the child's understanding of the story. Nurturing Narratives includes three levels of Tailored Stories. The story levels provide a basic model of language development that can guide interventionists in how to (a) modify language directed to the child to facilitate comprehension, (b) create developmentally appropriate stories, and (c) direct development of morpho-syntax.

The story levels broadly follow typical development. Linguistically, Level I focuses on establishing simple sentence patterns. Level II addresses expansion of noun and verb phrases, and Level III emphasizes complex sentences. Each Level also targets different narrative skills: Level I addresses interactive recounting of a simple event, Level II fosters independent retelling of single episode stories, and Level III adds emphasis on characters' thoughts and feelings in the story retelling.

The 4 M's, the second component of Nurturing Narratives, are key principles for implementing intervention. The 4 M's include **mentoring** the child and key adults in the child's life, creating **meaningful** and **manageable** learning content, and facilitating **mastery** learning. The 4 M's guide interventionists to address the child's unique learning needs by using scaffolds and language facilitation strategies that have been well documented in the literature (Paul, 2007).

The 4 M's blend social-pragmatics and Vygotskian strategies with applied behavior analysis. The first two are referred to as developmental interventions, whereas the third is a behavioral intervention. Ingersoll (2010) notes that "therapists from both perspectives often incorporate strategies from the other approach to improve child response" (p. 38).

The theoretical base for the components of the Nurturing Narratives model came from numerous writers and researchers. We would like to mention a few of these here. The use of stories as both the *context* and the *goal* for intervention was influenced by (Lyle,

Preface

2000) and others who stress the far-reaching importance of narrative in daily life. The writings of Judith Johnston (2006) and Marion Blank (2002) have been particularly influential. Both authors provide useful ideas on simplifying "the learning task through discourse engineering" (Johnston, 2006, p. 162).

"Links to Language" (Blank, McKirdy, & Payne, 1996) and "Teaching Tales" (Blank, McKirdy & Payne, 2000) influenced our ideas about language and narrative intervention for children with more significant language learning impairments. Arwood, Kaulitz, and Brown's (2009) book on visual thinking strategies provided information on how to create story illustrations that support children's understanding and learning. Norris and Hoffman's (1993) book on the whole-language intervention model was also quite influential. It illustrates how children discover the parts of language as they participate in larger "wholes," such as stories, and provided us with beginning support to use stories as a context for intervention.

Support for story-based language intervention is growing. Peterson (2010) reviewed eight studies on this type of intervention. Results showed that using repeated story retelling along with language facilitation procedures with children with language impairment (LI) may facilitate improvement in children's narrative skills and some components of their language. However, these studies unfortunately did not address children with severe receptive language problems.

As yet, the Nurturing Narratives model has not been empirically tested. However, guidelines for developing Tailored Stories and recommended language intervention strategies are based on evidence-based practices (EBP). (Please see Appendix F.) EBP is a framework for clinical decision making that entails "the integration of best research evidence with clinical expertise and patient values" (Sackett, Straus, Richardson, Rosenberg, & Haynes, 2000, p. 1).

To date, clinical results with many children have been favorable. Feedback about the Nurturing Narratives model from speech-language pathologists, teachers, and parents has also been positive. They often report that they have gained a better understanding of how to adapt their language to match the comprehension needs of individual children and have witnessed positive results (in terms of child responsiveness and engagement) from doing so. They also note that the Levels help them see where a given child is headed next on the continuum of language and narrative skills, which helps them make appropriate revisions in their own language use and the child's intervention plan as the child progresses.

In summary, while the developmental scheme of Nurturing Narratives has not been tested in its entirety, there is strong theoretical and empirical support for the teaching methods, and there is growing clinical support based on children's progress. Now that the framework has been "manualized," we invite you to join us in further investigating the Nurturing Narratives approach!

Foreword

You need only read the first page of Chapter 1 of *Nurturing Narratives* by Lauren Franke and Christine Durbin to understand why every speech-language pathologist, reading specialist, and special educator needs to read this book.

> "Narrative understanding is an important, if not *the* major, cognitive tool through which all human beings in all cultures make sense of the world" (Lyle, 2000, p. 9).

> "Longitudinal students have shown that narrative is the best predictor of outcomes for children with language disorders [including those with ASD] both in preschool (Bishop & Edmundson, 1987) and in elementary school" (Botting, Faragher, Know, Simkin, & Conti-Ramsden, 2001).

Narratives help our children and youth with ASD learn to:
- Relate the events of the day
- Learn literacy skills
- Problem solve
- Converse with others
- Take the perspective of others
- Develop comprehension skills
- Understand emotions
- Develop flexibility
- Engage in play and social interactions with others
- Develop vocabulary
- Understand and express cause and effect
- Sequence events
- Use appropriate grammar and syntax
- Increase self-esteem, confidence, and motivation
- And so forth …

Nurturing Narratives

In short, narrative skills help all of us, including our learners on the spectrum, to participate in the world with greater understanding.

And shouldn't this be our primary goal as educators and mentors?

Nurturing Narratives allows educational professionals to teach *literacy skills* in a manner that is compatible with the learning style of individuals with ASD. With this resource, literacy instruction in the classroom becomes a meaningful activity for our learners with ASD. They gain skills that will help them across their lifespan – from interacting with others on the playground to asking for help from a community member to discussing with a supervisor why a new procedure is needed to explaining effectively to a police officer why they were speeding.

Franke and Durbin, who have a unique understanding of school and clinical practice as well as the relevant research, present this evidence-based practice (see Appendix F) with step-by-step instructions. The book is comprehensive, yet easy to read and implement. At the risk of sounding cliché ... *this is a must-read that can change the lives of individuals with ASD and related disabilities.*

> – Brenda Smith Myles, Ph.D., a consultant with the Ziggurat Group, is the recipient of the 2004 Autism Society of America's Outstanding Professional Award and the 2006 Princeton Fellowship Award. She has written numerous articles and books on Asperger Syndrome and autism, including *Asperger Syndrome and Difficult Moments: Practical Solutions for Tantrums, Rage, and Meltdowns* (with Southwick) and *Asperger Syndrome and Adolescence: Practical Solutions for School Success* (with Adreon). The latter is the winner of the Autism Society of America's 2002 Outstanding Literary Work.

Section I: Introduction and Philosophy of Nurturing Narratives

Nurturing Narratives is a narrative-based language therapy approach that evolved during the quest to answer the question …

How do we as speech-language pathologists help children with the most challenging language impairments develop skills with one of the most challenging linguistic forms – the narrative?

Nurturing Narratives differs from existing narrative therapies. Most other approaches were developed for children who have language impairments that are milder or less complicated. Further, other narrative therapies are often based on teaching children the components of story grammar and start with fully developed stories. Nurturing Narratives, in contrast, was developed primarily for children who are not yet ready for a story-grammar approach. It begins with foundation skills for stories, followed by the developmental progression of narrative skills through three levels.

This book was written for speech-language pathologists (SLPs) and others who are mentored by SLPs. It is divided into three sections consisting of (a) an overview of the background and treatment principles of Nurturing Narratives, (b) guidelines for creating individualized Tailored Stories, and (c) guidelines for conducting Story Lessons (Nurturing Narratives intervention sessions) using evidence-based therapy techniques.

Section I reviews the background and principles of Nurturing Narratives. It includes information about:
- The importance, and challenges, of narratives
- Children with complicated language problems (CLP)
- Narrative-based language therapies
- The Nurturing Narratives model and theoretical foundation
- Principles of Nurturing Narratives intervention

Chapter 1

Nurturing Narratives

"To learn to speak is to learn to tell a story."

Le Guin (1989, p. 39)

The Importance of Narratives

People of all ages are inclined to perk up at the mere mention of the word *story*. The idea of story evokes thoughts of pleasure, leisure time, and entertainment. What does not come to mind for most of us is that the "story" is a critically important cognitive and communicative framework. Yet, it is! Based on a review of research on child development from several disciplines, Lyle (2000) reported that "narrative understanding is an important, if not *the* major, cognitive tool through which all human beings in all cultures make sense of the world. Human beings are predisposed to organize experience into narrative form" (p. 9). Hardy (1977) noted, "we dream, daydream, remember, anticipate, hope, despair, believe, doubt, plan, revise, criticize, construct, gossip, learn, hate and love by narrative" (p. 13).

Throughout our lives, stories pervade our days. Beginning early in life, stories play a pivotal role in children's development of self-concept, comprehension of their experiences, and interactions with family members and peers. Narratives are also important for school achievement. For example, longitudinal studies have shown that narrative is the best predictor of outcomes for children with language disorders both in preschool (Bishop & Edmundson, 1987) and in elementary school (Botting, Faragher, Knox, Simkin, & Conti-Ramsden, 2001). Children *need* narrative skills for social and academic success.

3

Problems with Stories

Surrounded by stories, children of all societies usually develop narrative skills in the course of participating in their day-to-day lives. But sadly, children with language learning problems do not develop narrative skills as readily. One reason for this is that narratives, being comprised of multiple related sentences, are innately complex and thus pose both receptive and expressive challenges for many children with language impairments.

Even Simple Narratives Are Complex

"[Stories] move children beyond the sentence into larger units of language, and into the challenges of language use in context."

Johnston (2006, p. 145)

This statement goes to the heart of the problems that stories pose for children who struggle with language at the word and sentence level, who have difficulty using language to communicate in social contexts, or both.

To comprehend a story, a child needs to have some knowledge of the topic on which the story is based (e.g., building a snowman, shopping for a birthday present, fire fighting) as well as an understanding of the words and sentence patterns used in the story. Once the individual words and sentences have been processed, the child must synthesize them into a meaningful whole. If the story happens to contain challenging vocabulary, unfamiliar sentence forms, and/or inferences (most stories do), the job of gleaning meaning from it can become daunting, if not impossible, for a child with a language impairment.

To retell a story, the child must first understand it. Then comes the task of retrieving the needed words and sentence patterns, putting them in correct sequence, and tying them together cohesively and coherently.

Creating a story is even more complicated than retelling one. Take the following account told by a preschooler to her mother ...

"I made a hat at school today. I painted it pink and purple. It was pretty!"

4

This early personal narrative reflects several coordinated components. First the child needed to tap her store of event knowledge and call up a generalized script for arts and crafts projects. She then used this script to help her organize her story and remember relevant vocabulary. She also used her autobiographical memory to recall pertinent details of the specific event about which she was reporting.

Although the story is made up of simple sentences, it also contains some elements of linguistic complexity – it is told in the past tense with one regular and two irregular verbs, and contains a prepositional phrase, three adjectives, and an adverb. The sentences are linked together thematically and they are sequenced correctly. The pronoun *it* in the second and third sentences successfully references the noun *hat* in the first sentence. The story begins with character and setting information, which sets the stage for the listener to understand the details that follow, and so on.

Stories Told by Children with Language Impairments

"Jumping Around and Leaving Things Out" is how Johnston (2006, p. 140) titled a discussion of stories told by children with specific language impairment (SLI). In that discussion, Johnston reported on a study by Miranda, McCabe, and Bliss (1998), in which personal narratives of children with "relatively severe SLI" were compared with language-matched younger children. Results of the study indicated, "The children with language impairment included more irrelevant content, skipped over and reordered more key events, left more of the story implicit, and made more reformulations than did the younger controls" (Johnston, pp. 140-141).

Similarly, Ukrainetz and Gillam (2009) reviewed studies comparing the narrative performance of children with SLI with those of typically developing children and reported that the narrative retells of children with SLI are "shorter and contain simpler syntax, more grammatical errors, and less diverse and sophisticated vocabulary" (p. 984). They also noted that the oral narratives of these children are "less fluent, with more verbal mazes … and include fewer semantic propositions, more meaning departures and more extraneous material" (p. 984).

Given the importance and complexity of stories, children with language impairments clearly need interventions to help them acquire narrative skills.

Narrative-Based Intervention

Figure 1.1. Story-centered therapy.

Centering therapy on stories can be quite efficacious. Doing so lends itself to interweaving multiple goals into one integrated whole. Also, certain aspects of narrative can enhance comprehension or acquisition of others.. For example, a story that contains a familiar story event and familiar syntax can bootstrap learning of new vocabulary; a story with a well-known plot and easily understood text can facilitate comprehension of story characters' perspectives, and so on.

Children tend to find stories fun. An engaging story can entice a child to interact with the storyteller. As such, stories can generate opportunities for interaction and collaboration and a whole host of social, play, and communication skills. Then in a playful, interactive context, there are numerous ways stories can be told and retold, altered and enhanced, to create multiple opportunities for practicing language targets.

As noted, most narrative intervention programs focus on teaching children the components of story grammar (characters, setting, problem, solution, etc.). While such programs have been shown to be effective in facilitating narrative skills in children with language impairments (Hayward & Schneider, 2000; Kaderavek & Hunt, 2005; Klecan-Aker, 1993; Swanson, Fey & Mills, 2005), some children do not have the requisite linguistic and metacognitive skills to benefit from intervention based on a story grammar model. A different narrative therapy approach is needed for these children, who often have more *complicated* language problems. This is where Nurturing Narratives comes in.

Children with Complicated Language Problems

There is a subgroup of children with language impairments who have what we call "complicated language problems" (CLP). These are children whose communication problems are compounded by issues such as cognitive challenges, problems with social relatedness, attention deficits, emotional regulation difficulties, and others. These children may have diagnoses such as autism spectrum disorders (ASD), intellectual disability, or attention deficit/ hyperactivity disorder (ADHD).

Due to the complicated nature of their communication and learning difficulties, children with CLP are at a particularly high risk for missing out on both the joys and benefits of stories. Making stories – with all their cognitive, social, and linguistic benefits – accessible to children with CLP is the focus of Nurturing Narratives.

Pete is one of many children who have significantly influenced the development of this approach. His story, which follows, helps illustrate how challenging it can be to accurately tailor a narrative therapy program to a child with significant developmental challenges but how doing so can considerably promote more meaningful and rewarding participation in a social-communicative world to which the child previously had very little access.

Pete's Story

The Starting Point

When he was 8 years old, Pete's case was transferred to Kate for speech and language therapy. At that time, a recent assessment indicated that Pete's cognitive and language skills were at approximately the 18- to 24-month level. Although he demonstrated some autistic traits, a diagnosis of autism was ruled out due to his relative strength in social relatedness (however, he was later diagnosed with autism at age 10).

Pete generally spoke in one- to two-word phrases, primarily to request wants and occasionally to comment on something of interest like an airplane flying overhead. He was very reliant on his mother speaking for him.

Pete was rather isolated socially; he showed no interest in other children and had no interaction with his classmates. However, he was happy and playful with his parents, and particularly enjoyed play with them that involved chasing and tickling. When a familiar adult greeted Pete, he smiled brightly and said "hi," but when the other person began to say more to him, Pete started squirming and looking ill at ease. Before long, he quietly slipped away from the interaction. Most of the language around and directed to Pete appeared to be incomprehensible to him. Even though there were indications that Pete liked social interaction, the verbal world seemed to make him uncomfortable, and he avoided it.

Pete's Response to Language Therapy

Kate and Pete's parents wanted Pete to be able to have more meaningful communicative exchanges with the people in his life. Kate launched an intensive, structured therapy and home program with Pete that focused on expanding his fund of syntax.

For a while this approach seemed to hold promise. Pete demonstrated progress in structured therapy activities; he was able to imitate sentences of increasing length and complexity while watching Kate act out the sentences with toy figures. However, his mother, Alice, reported that Pete still rarely spoke at home and only spoke in one- to two-word utterances when he did. Kate and Alice stepped up efforts to facilitate Pete's use of the new sentence patterns in meaningful communicative contexts, but little progress was observed. When Pete's progress in therapy sessions plateaued, and he began to demonstrate increased problems with attention and focus and decreased compliance, Kate knew it was time for a change of plan, but she was not sure what that should be.

Introduction of Stories

Kate had never considered Pete a candidate for narrative therapy. However, one day she decided to try a simple story with him – a two-picture sequence story about a dog looking at, and then eating food from, his dog bowl. She worked on his imitation of the story sentences and facilitation of spontaneous language about the story pictures, first with, then without, the pictures showing. Each of these activities was difficult for Pete and required significant scaffolding from Kate. She was not even sure that Pete understood the story (his mother said he had never had a pet), but he was fairly engaged, so Kate decided to experiment with narrative therapy with Pete. A few weeks later she got a call from Pete's mother …

A First

Alice telephoned to tell Kate that Pete had come home that day and told her about something that had happened at school. She said he only said a couple of words, and she had to do a lot of digging to figure out what he was talking about, but this had been the first time Pete had ever come home and tried to tell her about something that had happened that day. Hearing this report, Kate became more convinced that she should continue incorporating stories in Pete's therapy.

Simplifying ... and Simplifying Some More

As Pete continued to significantly struggle with two-picture stories, Kate progressively simplified them in different ways in her successive sessions with him. First she began acting out the stories with toys so Pete could see the link between the actions. Next, she used simpler language in the story text, then less language. Finally, she began altering stories so that they only contained language in Pete's repertoire, which included sentence patterns he had successfully imitated in their earlier syntax-focused therapy. Kate also began basing Pete's stories only on topics that were very familiar to him.

Eventually, Kate simplified Pete's stories to the point where they were very short – three to four sentences long. One story was, "Here is a boy. He is swinging. He is happy." With such stories, Pete was able to imitate the sentences, act out the story using toy miniatures, and match the actions to the text as Kate told the story. With moderate scaffolding, he could retell the story on his own as he acted it out with the toys. Pete was attentive and engaged. Kate found out that Pete could persist in the face of difficulties, a trait she had not seen in him before. He came to know that the final expectation was for him to tell the story all by himself. Often when he reached that goal, he beamed even before she praised him.

Kate had finally found stories that "fit" Pete. At the end of their sessions, she drew simple pictures of the stories for Pete to take home and use to help him tell the stories to his family.

Progression of Pete's Narrative Therapy

Kate began to add elements of complexity to stories for Pete, such as a new vocabulary word, grammatical structure, or sentence pattern, one at a time. She also scaffolded Pete's retelling of stories in the past tense, without visual or verbal cues. She had to be careful not to add too much complexity at the same time so Pete would not become overwhelmed and disorganized.

Over time, Pete was able to retell longer and more complex stories; he reached the point where he could retell from memory an 8- to 10-sentence story (after practicing it several times) that contained one to two characters, a simple problem and solution, and a feeling response of the character(s). One such story was, "Here is a boy. He has an airplane. Oh no, the airplane is broken! The boy is sad. He is giving the airplane to Dad. Dad is fixing the airplane. The boy is playing with the airplane. Now the boy is happy."

Addition of Personal Narratives

At Kate's request, Alice began to help Pete prepare a personal narrative to bring to his language therapy session each week. She drew simple pictures to help Pete remember and correctly sequence the story. Pete's earliest personal narratives went something like, "I went to Olive Garden. I ate spaghetti. It was good." Alice helped Pete practice telling his stories a few times before his sessions with Kate. "Rehearsing" the stories enabled Pete to be able to independently tell them to others, an experience he had never had before.

At first, Pete used his good rote memory skill to memorize the story sentences. He told his stories rather flatly in a monotone voice, seemingly without any meaning being attached to the stories for him. But after a while, Pete, typically a passive non-initiator, started to arrive at the sessions and request his story pictures from his mother. He referenced his pictures, but began directing the "telling" to Kate. He used more intonation and smiled at appropriate points in the story. He was more engaged and seemed surer of himself.

After Pete had been bringing stories to tell Kate for a while, she started telling him stories about her experiences, too. She told simple stories using language similar to that in Pete's stories about events she thought he could understand. Simple conversational exchanges were scripted into the exchange of stories. Kate wanted Pete to experience taking part in exchanges that were akin to what happens in conversation between friends.

Symbolic Play

Pete demonstrated an interest in cooking, and his first pretend play involved toy food and dishes. For quite a while this was limited to just two routines, which Pete would repeat over and over without variation – pretending to pour juice in a cup and drink it, and putting toy food on a plate and pretending to cut and then eat it.

Kate had incorporated the food preparation and eating theme into several stories for Pete. Once, early in Pete's narrative therapy, she gave him a basket of toys that contained toys for a "kitchen story" mixed in with other toys. He said nothing, but he did pull out all of the appropriate toys. He sat two dolls at a picnic table and then proceeded to place all the dishes and food items on the table. When he ran out of space, he placed the items on the table benches, and when they filled up, he stacked the food toys. Once the food toys were all piled, he stacked the rest of the toys from the basket on top of the food toys. The only schema Pete demonstrated for interacting with these toys was stacking.

A few months later, Kate assessed Pete's spontaneous play skills again. She gave him a similar basket of toys and asked him to tell a kitchen story. Pete took a toy boy, spaghetti, pan, and stove out of the basket. He acted out a simple story as he narrated it. Then he took out a toy girl, a bottle of soda, and a cup, and created a second simple story with them. Kate asked him to draw the story pictures and tell his story again. Pete's story and pictures are shown in Figure 1.2.

"Here is a kitchen.   Here is a boy and a girl.   The boy is cooking the spaghetti.

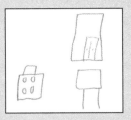

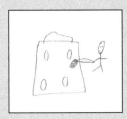

The boy is eating the spaghetti.   The girl is pouring the   The girl is drinking the cola.
It is delicious!   cola.   She is happy!"

Figure 1.2. **Pete's kitchen story.**

Kate had never asked Pete to create his own story before. She was very pleased that his stories indicated that he had internalized a simple story framework, namely, "a character, action and feeling or coda."

In the Game

During one visit to Pete's classroom, Kate observed him during recess time. Pete went to the basketball court. (This was reportedly a new development. For the past several years, Pete had always played on the climbing structure by himself during recess.) Someone threw the ball to Pete early on, but then he was left out of the game. He was not successful in communicating his desire to play, and he started to get upset. Kate told him to say, "Give the ball to me." He said this several times, and finally the ball was thrown to him. He got to shoot, and he was happy.

Recess was followed by a quiet work period in the classroom. Kate asked Pete's teacher if she could work with Pete to make a story about what had happened on the playground. The teacher agreed and said he could then tell it to the class. Kate drew simple stick figure drawings to help aid Pete's recall and telling of the story. Using the pictures as a reference, Pete was able to tell the story by himself. His class was very impressed and praised him. They had never heard him say so much! Pete seemed quite pleased with himself.

> "I was playing basketball. I said, 'Give the ball to me.' Aaron gave the ball to me. I was shooting the ball. I was happy!"

Pete's teacher and aide were receptive to learning how to help Pete create simple stories like this and facilitate opportunities for him to tell his stories to others.

Christmas Salad

Pete's mother reported that Pete's family spent a lot of time with their extended family, but that Pete mostly kept to himself during these gatherings. Kate suggested having Pete tell one of his stories at a family meal and Alice liked the idea. On Christmas day, Pete helped his mom prepare a salad for the dinner. Then the two of them created a story about it for Pete to tell the family. Alice later reported that Pete used the story pictures, did a great job of telling the story to the family, and smiled widely when they applauded him.

> "I was making salad with Mom. I was tearing the lettuce. I was putting the lettuce in the bowl. I was cutting the cheese. I was putting the cheese in the bowl. The salad was done!"

Two Final Stories About Pete

Kate did not see Pete for therapy over the summer months. When he came back for his first session in September, he met her at the door. He held up a little toy flashlight and said something like, "It's broken. The flashlight is broken. Miss Lee gave me the flashlight. It's broken." Kate looked at his mom in surprise. Alice said, "It started over the summer. He's talking all the time now."

Alice had continued to develop personal narratives with Pete through the summer, and he had a whole stack of stories to tell Kate. He started with the picture cues his mother had drawn and the text they had practiced, but for some stories he was able to add some new ideas of his own.

Several weeks later when Alice was volunteering at Pete's school, she saw him walking down the hall with his class. There was a child sitting on the floor in the middle of the hall. As Alice watched, Pete pointed at the child and said to the girl next to him, "Look at that." Pete, who had been isolated from his peers for years, not only observed and talked about another child, he directed his comment to a peer!

Pete's language skills will never develop to a high level, and he will likely always need for people in his life to support many of his communicative interactions. However, it does appear that narrative intervention has helped him move from a place where he once avoided the verbal world to a place where he is learning the fun and usefulness of communication, and has thus, in some way, improved the quality of his life.

Nurturing Narratives

Nurturing Narratives is an intervention model that involves systematically facilitating mastery of new language skills during engaging, interactive story-based activities. Teaching procedures mix developmental social pragmatic strategies and applied behavioral analysis.

The Nurturing Narratives approach is described in the context of speech and language therapy sessions in which two types of stories – personal narratives and fictional stories – are the focus. Both types of stories are individualized to match a child's levels of cognitive and linguistic development and address the child's language intervention goals. These stories are called **Tailored Stories.** The therapy sessions are referred to as **Story Lessons**.

Skills that can be targeted during Story Lessons include:

- Social communication and conversation

- Grammar, syntax, and vocabulary

- Story comprehension and retelling

- Interactive symbolic play

- Theory of mind

The Nurturing Narratives model is divided into three levels of intervention that each targets a different level of story complexity:

Level I: Events focuses on short, simple Tailored Stories that are based on familiar events in the child's life. These are considered entry-level stories.

Level II: Surprises. Here the stories begin to include problems and solutions; causal and temporal relationships are highlighted.

Level III: Theory of Mind. At this level, Tailored Stories increase in complexity, to include focus on understanding the story characters' thoughts and perspectives.

The components of the Nurturing Narratives model are summarized in Figure 1.3. For a more detailed summary, see "Nurturing Narratives at-a-Glance" on page 15.

Nurturing Narratives Principles +	Tailored Stories =	Nurturing Narratives Intervention
The "4 M's"	Guidelines for creating 3 Levels of Tailored Stories:	Story Lessons (2 Segments)
• **M**entor the child and the child's communication partners • Create language learning activities which are **M**eaningful and **M**anageable for the child • Foster **M**astery of new skills	I. Events II. Surprises III. Theory of Mind	**Sharing Personal Narratives** Child and adult exchange stories about their recent experiences in a conversational context **Understanding and Retelling Stories** Story comprehension and retelling are addressed in the context of varied, interactive story repetitions

Figure 1.3. Nurturing Narratives model.

Column 1 in Figure 1.3 represents the core principles of Nurturing Narratives, which are embodied in the "4 M's," a set of guidelines for furthering the language comprehension and communication skills of children with CLP. The 4 M's are reviewed in Chapter 2.

Column 2 focuses on the central teaching content, Tailored Stories. The components of Tailored Stories and guidelines for creating individualized stories are discussed in Chapters 3 and 5.

The principles of Nurturing Narratives intervention and Tailored Stories come together in Story Lessons, which are story-based intervention sessions (see column 3). Implementation of intervention sessions is the topic of Chapter 7.

The Nurturing Narratives model is based on a solid theoretical foundation (see Table 1.1), which makes it particularly relevant and critical in an educational climate that mandates evidence-based practice.

Table 1.1

Theoretical Foundation for Nurturing Narratives

Learning Context	+	Content	=	Intervention
The 4 M's		**Tailored Stories**		**Story Lesson**
• Dynamic Tricky Mix Theory (Nelson, Craven, Xuan, & Arkenber, 2004) • Social Interaction Model (Vygotsky, 1978) • Situated Pragmatics Model (Duchan,1997) • Participation Model (Beukelman & Mirenda, 1998; Kaderavek & Rabidoux, 2004)		• Information Processing Model (Just & Carpenter, 1992; Lahey & Bloom, 1994) • Event Knowledge (Nelson, 1986, 1996) • Client-Specific Experimental Approach (Hedge & Maul, 2006)		• Developmentally Based Social Pragmatic Strategies • (MacDonald, 1989; Mahoney & Perales, 2003; Prizant, Wetherby, Rubin, & Laurent, 2006; Sussman, 1999) • Applied Behavior Analysis (Baer, Wolf, & Risley, 1968) • Contingent Language Facilitation Procedures (Fey, 1986; Leonard, 1998; McCauley & Fey, 2006)

Table 1.2

Nurturing Narratives at-a-Glance

4 M's – NN Principles: Mentor – Meaningful – Manageable – Mastery

Tailored Stories: 3 Levels of Individualized Stories That Are "Tailored" To:
• be meaningful and manageable for the child • address the child's therapy goals and interests

Story Lessons: Narrative-Based Intervention Sessions (2 Segments)		
SEGMENT	**1. Sharing Personal Narratives**	**2. Understanding and Retelling Stories**
Story Type	Personal narratives	Fictional stories
Description	Child and adult exchange stories about their recent experiences in a conversational context	Story comprehension and retelling are addressed in the context of varied, interactive story repetitions
Key Focus	Expansion of pragmatic skills	Expansion of receptive and expressive language
Similarities	• Top priority: Engagement • Therapy goals are addressed in meaningful, naturalistic contexts • Same level of story complexity, support and "demand" (i.e., expectation for independent performance) • Opportunities for repeated story practice with scaffolded support	

Nurturing Narratives Levels		
	Tailored Stories personal narratives & fictional stories	**Story Lessons** narrative-based intervention sessions
	Level of Story Complexity	**Primary Focus**
Level I **Events**	**Low** Simple stories are based on familiar events and routines or recent personal experiences	• Engagement, joint attention, and reciprocal interaction • Interactive retelling of simple stories • Automaticity of basic sentence patterns • Internalization of a simple story framework
Level II **Surprises**	**Moderate** Stories contain problems and solutions	• Early conversation skills • Independent retelling of stories in past tense • Expression of temporal & causal relationships in stories
Level III **Theory of** **Mind**	**High** Stories focus on characters' thoughts and perspectives	• Independence in simple conversations • Theory of mind skills • Expanded repertoire of complex sentences

Chapter 2

The 4 M's – The Key Principles of Nurturing Narratives

"Successful learning ... always involves what we term a Tricky Mix of multiple, positive, and converging cognitive, communicative, social, emotional, and self-esteem factors."

Nelson, Welsh, Camerata, Heimann, & Tjus (2001, p. 159)

The combination of critical elements needed for learning to occur is both complex and elusive. Finding the right blend of components is particularly crucial for children with CLP, whose compounded learning problems make them much more likely to miss a learning opportunity than their typically developing peers. As we strive to bridge the learning obstacles of children with CLP with the goals we want them to reach in intervention, we have found the 4 M's to be a useful reference and guide.

The 4 M's
• **Mentoring** the child and key adults in the child's life
• Creating **meaningful** and **manageable** learning content
• Facilitating **mastery** learning

M 1: Mentor

The term *mentor* implies that the interventionist will remain finely tuned to the child and scaffold learning activities to facilitate his meaningful progress and sense of accomplishment. In Nurturing Narratives, the interventionist's role involves mentoring the child and others who are in a position to impact the child's language learning.

Mentoring the Child
• **Foster the child's engagement** • **Scaffold learning**
Mentoring Key Adults in the Child's Life
• **Create multiple environments that facilitate language learning** • **Provide frequent, varied opportunities for practicing new skills**

Mentoring the Child

1. Foster the Child's Engagement

Some children with CLP are challenging to engage and motivate. For many, problems with receptive and/or expressive language cause them to feel uncomfortable or overwhelmed when others attempt to interact with them verbally. Children with ASD often demonstrate difficulty with social engagement and children with ADD or ADHD struggle with issues of arousal, attention, and focus.

While there are many reasons why it can be challenging to engage children with CLP in language-related activities, it is essential that we do just that! When engagement is absent, the potential for learning is decreased at best and may not exist at all. *When children are engaged, they are in a readiness state for learning.*

The Interventionist-Child Relationship

Establishing a relationship with the child that is warm, positive, and fun is the first step in facilitating engagement. In Nurturing Narratives, we want to foster the child's sense of security and enjoyment as well as willingness and confidence to participate in interactions and activities that promote development of skills for effective communication.

The 4 M's – The Key Principles of Nurturing Narratives

We aim to establish an unspoken pact with the child that certain expectations will be met on both sides. We want to build the child's trust that we will not present challenges that he* is unable to meet, and that when our help is required to meet a challenge, we will provide all the support the child needs to succeed. For the child's part, we hope that he will be motivated to put forth the effort needed to meet our reasonable demands.

Emotion and Learning

"Emotion plays a … positive role [in human learning] in that the stronger the emotion connected to an experience, the stronger the memory of that experience. Chemicals in the brain send a message to the rest of the brain: "This information is important. Remember it." Thus, **when we are able to add emotional input into learning experiences to make them more meaningful and exciting, the brain deems the information more important and retention is increased** [emphasis added]."

Wolfe & Brandt (1998, p. 5)

In Nurturing Narratives we infuse learning activities with emotion in a variety of ways. During interactions with the child:

- We establish an inviting interpersonal relationship with the child to facilitate positive feelings and memories associated with interacting with us and with learning.

- We use emotion to communicate our confidence in the child's abilities and inspire motivation to rise to the challenge as we scaffold the child's retelling of the story.

We also include emotional content in almost all Nurturing Narratives stories, even the simplest ones:

- A typical story in Level I might be …
    This is a girl. She is sliding. She is happy!

- Stories are also invested with emotion when they have unexpected turns or surprises ...
    Here is a boy. He has an ice cream cone. Oh no!
    The ice cream is falling! The boy is sad!

    or

    Here is a boy. He has an ice cream cone.
    Uh oh! The ice cream is falling! Oh look!
    The boy is catching the ice cream! Whew! He is so happy!

For ease of reading, throughout the book, we are using the pronoun he to refer to children, and the pronoun she to refer to the adult interventionist.

- We imbue *telling* of the story with elements of emotion, too. Stories are told with heightened affect and exaggerated intonation to convey our own interest and excitement about the story.

> **When we are successful in facilitating the association of emotion with the learning experience, we increase the likelihood of the learning material being meaningfully remembered.**

2. Scaffold Learning

One of the primary roles of a mentor is to *scaffold* the child's learning. "In scaffolding, the adult guides and supports the child's learning by building on what the child is able to do … Effective scaffolding is flexible, responsive to the child, draws on a variety of strategies, and varies across cultures" (O'Connor, Notari-Syverson, & Vadasy, 2005, p. 12).

Scaffolds range from those involving high levels of support and low levels of demand to the inverse – low levels of support with high levels of demand. Scaffolding is a very dynamic process. A mentor continually adjusts scaffolding to provide the support the child needs while facilitating the child's progress toward independent performance of the skill.

Two Types of Scaffolds

According to Ukrainetz (2006), "SLPs can provide structural scaffolds through the careful selection of materials, order of presentation, tools, and modifying environmental conditions" (p. 37). **Structural scaffolds** are used to construct and arrange the learning content and context to facilitate the learning process. **Interactive scaffolds** are used to respond to the child's needs in the moment in order to keep the learning activity manageable for the child. Interactive scaffolding is also referred to as *responsive scaffolding* or *situational support*.

Ideally, one offers just the right amount of scaffolding to help the child move past a comprehension or production problem that he cannot hurdle without some assistance. The goal is to reduce scaffolding over time as the child demonstrates the ability to understand/perform with greater degrees of independence.

Table 2.1 lists examples of three types of interactive scaffolds.

The 4 M's – The Key Principles of Nurturing Narratives

Table 2.1

Three Types of Interactive Scaffolds

Types of Facilitative Moves Used in Interactive Scaffolding		
Response Facilitations	**Linguistic Facilitations**	**Regulatory Facilitations**
• Wait for a response • Model the response • Repeat and emphasize • Cue through physical signals • Pause before providing the answer • Provide part of the answer • Provide the answer and have the student repeat it	• Model (provide in advance) • Expand (add adult syntactic/semantic element) • Extend (add to topic) • Recast (change the syntactic structure) • Use vertical structuring (combine two student utterances) • Use build-up/breakdown (model both telegraphic and complete sentences) • Use focused contrast (pair the error and correction) • Redirect (show student how to ask or tell another person)	• Maintain awareness and acceptance of the goal • Highlight importance of content • Relate content to past knowledge • Comment on student performance • Inhibit impulsive responses • Aid selective and sustained attention • Help student manage challenge • Review cumulative performance • Comment on task similarities

Note. From "Assessment and Intervention Within a Contextualized Skill Framework," by T. A. Ukrainetz, 2006, *Contextualized Language Intervention: Scaffolding Pre-K-12 Literacy Achievement* (p. 39), T. A. Ukrainetz (Ed.), Austin, TX: PRO-ED. Copyright 2006 by PRO-ED, Inc. Reprinted with permission.

Mentoring Key Adults in the Child's Life

1. Create Environments That Facilitate Language Learning

Nelson et al. (2004) suggested that long-term, persistent language delays result in part from language partners' failure to use language that can be effectively processed or understood by children with language impairments. An important aspect of the SLP's role, therefore, is to teach others in the child's life how to create day-to-day interactions for the child that are meaningful and facilitate language growth.

2. Provide Frequent and Varied Opportunities for Practicing New Skills

Children with CLP generally need intensive practice to meet their language goals. In Nurturing Narratives we train others to help children gain this practice while communicating meaningfully with a variety of communicative partners in a range of contexts. When we are successful in doing this, the child stands to achieve significantly better outcomes from the intervention.

M 2: Meaningful

> "Trying to drill higher-level learning into immature brains may force them to perform with lower-level systems and thus impair the skill in question."
>
> Healy (1999, p. 69)

The primary teaching content in Nurturing Narratives is Tailored Stories, stories that children with CLP can relate to and understand. While this seems an obvious goal, the importance of it cannot be overemphasized, especially for children with more severe learning challenges.

It is not uncommon for children who have significant cognitive and linguistic impairments to be presented with learning activities that contain language and concepts that are beyond their level of understanding. Discussing the calendar during Circle Time may be an example of this for some children. Reading a story about a snowman to children who have never seen snow is another. In cases like these, the expectation, or hope, is that the children will glean meaning from what they are exposed to at the level they are capable.

Nurturing Narratives is based on a very different premise. We believe one needs to create teaching content that is highly meaningful for children with CLP in order to truly promote their learning. The more limited the child's ability, the more challenging and more necessary this task becomes.

Meanings of "Meaningful"

When we want to make a story meaningful for a child who has an identified language learning problem, we usually think in terms of simplifying the language. This helps to make the story more understandable, but there are other aspects of "meaningful" that we also need to think about.

The 4 M's – The Key Principles of Nurturing Narratives

Consider the following children, each of whom has a different presentation of CLP.

- Carmen, a 10-year-old child with moderate cognitive and linguistic challenges, understands and uses simple and compound sentences but only understands language that relates to experiences she has had or has directly observed in her daily life.

- Cognitively intact, 4-year-old Sam has limited vocabulary and is struggling with early sentence patterns, but he understands the basic concepts in stories about space travel and good guys versus bad guys. He is attracted to these topics and finds stories about daily events uninteresting. When he is bored, he tends to become fidgety and unfocused.

- Chloe has a diagnosis of high-functioning autism/Asperger Syndrome. She attends a regular third-grade class and is quite verbal. She loves to read stories at her age level but usually does not understand the characters' feelings and motives and often misses information that is inferred.

These three children have very different story comprehension issues. Carmen has limited knowledge of events that stories are based on. Sam has much more extensive event knowledge than Carmen, but he has trouble attending to stories that do not relate to his interests. And Chloe's comprehension difficulties relate to her poor social cognition and verbal reasoning skills. **"Meaningful" stories for each of these children would be quite different from each other.**

Tailored Stories

Tailored Stories are central to the Nurturing Narratives approach. They are a form of scaffolding in that they are written to aid or enhance processing. The closer we can match stories to a child's strengths, needs, and interests, the more meaningful the stories will be for that child. Chapters 3-5 are devoted to creating Tailored Stories.

M 3: Manageable

"If there is a finite amount of mental energy available at any one moment, a task that requires greater concentration or efficiency may use enough of this capacity that little remains for work on a second task. When the traffic is heavy, it is hard to talk and drive."

Johnston (2006, p. 54)

In working with children with CLP, we have found that most problem behaviors are due to the fact that we are presenting tasks that are too difficult for them. Now when we observe behavioral difficulties such as inattention, avoidance, or aggression, one of the first things we do is attempt to revise the task so that it better matches the child's abilities and mental resources. **When we are successful in creating learning activities that are manageable for the child, behavior issues often decrease or disappear, and engagement and motivation tend to increase.**

Key Strategies for Creating Manageable Learning Activities

Current theories and research (see below) indicate the following strategies are effective for creating manageable learning activities.

1. Stay Within the Child's Zone of Proximal Development

The zone of proximal development (ZPD) was described by Vygotsky (1978) as the range between what the child is able to do independently and the upper level of performance the child can attain when provided with adult support. Brown and Reeve (1987) referred to this range as the "bandwidth of competence" (p. 177).

Learning activities should be designed to focus on achievement of only the skills that fall within the range of what is meaningful and manageable for the child with adult scaffolding. As Johnston (2006) noted, "When instructional experiences are designed to advance the child's knowledge one step beyond its current level, learning is more likely to occur" (p. 158).

2. Intersperse New Learning with Old

Research has shown that children with ASD and other disabilities learn new skills at an increased rate when previously mastered tasks are interspersed with tasks focused on acquisition of new skills (Chong & Carr, 2005; Dunlap & Koegel, 1980; Koegel & Koegel, 1986). We have found that some children with CLP are more likely to stay attentive and engaged and

24

to master new skills at a quicker pace when approximately 80% of the material in a learning activity is "review" or readily understood, and 20% is challenging; however, the ratio of review and challenging material which works best will vary from child to child.

3. Provide Side Lessons as Needed

Despite our best efforts to present learning material that is reasonably within the child's grasp, there will be times when the meaning of a new word or concept or the production of a new linguistic pattern proves to be particularly daunting for the child in the context of a story. At moments like these, one must decide whether to revise or eliminate that item or whether to conduct a Side Lesson.

Side Lessons involve taking a side step, so to speak, away from the story-based activity to provide more in-depth instruction and/or practice with the challenging element. At the end of a Side Lesson, the new information or skill is reintegrated into the story-based activity rather than leaving it as a splinter skill that the child may or may not know how to integrate with his existing knowledge.

While Side Lessons may be needed at times, their use should be relatively infrequent. If multiple Side Lessons are needed during a particular story, the content of the story is likely at a level that is too high for the child and should be revised or eliminated.

M 4: Mastery

A child will probably not spontaneously demonstrate a new skill that requires significant effort to perform. Similarly, new knowledge is not likely to be integrated with existing knowledge if the child's understanding of it is still vague.

Mastery in Nurturing Narratives refers to solid attainment of target skills. That is, the Nurturing Narratives model is designed to help children with CLP reach a level where they "own" their new knowledge and skills and are able to use them purposefully with relative ease.

According to Johnston (2006), there is evidence to indicate that mental representations of newly acquired language continue to evolve and strengthen.

> Researchers characterize these later changes in different ways depending
> upon their theories and emphasis areas. The connectionists talk about the
> decreases in the level of activation needed to energize a scheme; the memory

folks talk about improved access to stored language representations. In the traditional practice of speech therapy, there is the notion of stimulability; in more recent practice we have the notion of automaticity or mastery learning. What drives all of this theorizing is the observation that the ability to use what we know improves systematically with time, practice, and further learning. (p. 127)

After reviewing research on "what works in treatment," Ukrainetz (2006) identified four critical elements of effective treatment. She summarized these elements in the acronym RISE, which stands for "*R*epeated opportunities, delivered in an *I*ntensive schedule, of *S*ystematically support[ed] *E*xplicit skill instruction" (p. 291).

In Nurturing Narratives, stories are repeated numerous times as comprehension and story retelling are scaffolded. The story presentations are varied to facilitate the child's continued interest and to help network the new information in multiple modalities (e.g., visual, auditory, proprioceptive). Intensity of practice is also accomplished as the child practices retelling stories to other communicative partners in different settings. Children are intensively exposed to new vocabulary and syntactic patterns in stories and Side Lessons as needed to master them. Likewise, they are repeatedly exposed to certain types of stories until they are able to internalize their structure.

Effect of Mastery on the Child

When children are able to fluently retell a story, a number of things can happen. The children can more easily recall the story at a later time. They may integrate new vocabulary and syntactic patterns they have learned into their existing repertoires. Having a fluent story to tell sets the stage for participating in the type of story-sharing interactions most people engage in several times a day. The children may not resist requests to tell the story to others; in fact, they might enjoy the exchange. After a number of positive experiences with telling others stories, the children may begin to associate favorable feelings and memories with the event of story sharing and become motivated to seek more social interactions. They also might begin to try to tell stories of their own.

One of the best byproducts of a child "mastering" a story is the positive effect it can have on the child's self-esteem, confidence, and motivation. With mastery comes a sense of accomplishment. We want to make learning activities relevant and manageable with a mixture of trust, fun, and work so children learn to take on challenges, feel proud of their hard work, and experience the benefits communicating.

Section II:
Tailored Stories

Given that even simple stories are inherently complex, it is difficult to find stories to use in language therapy that are meaningful and manageable for children with CLP. This search for appropriate stories was the impetus for developing a system for creating Tailored Stories. Tailored Stories are stories that are individualized to address the child's language therapy goals and match his levels of cognitive and linguistic functioning, background knowledge, and interests.

Tailored Stories
• Match the child's levels of cognitive and linguistic functioning • Address the child's language goals

Section II consists of information and tools for creating Tailored Stories. These include:

- A review of the Tailored Story Components – cognitive and linguistic elements that influence story complexity (Chapter 3)

- Suggestions for preschool-level assessment of the Tailored Story Components (text boxes at the end of the discussion of each Tailored Story Component)

- Evidence-based support for the Tailored Story Components (Appendix F)

- An overview of the Nurturing Narratives Levels – three levels of Tailored Stories and narrative-based intervention for children with CLP (Chapter 4)

- Guidelines for creating Tailored Stories with samples of two types of stories – personal narratives and fictional stories – at each of the Nurturing Narratives Levels (Chapter 5)

Chapter 3

Tailored Story Components

As a first step in creating Tailored Stories, it is helpful to consider the components of Tailored Stories – the cognitive and linguistic elements that influence story complexity (see Table 3.1). The more familiar the interventionist is with the elements that can interfere with effective processing of stories, the easier it is to identify and revise them when they create stumbling blocks for a child during story-based intervention.

Table 3.1

Tailored Story Components

TAILORED STORY COMPONENTS					
Elements of Cognitive Complexity			**Elements of Linguistic Complexity**		
Event Knowledge	Contextualization	Story Memory	Story Text	Syntax	Semantics

A key consideration when creating Tailored Stories involves the notion of **processing demand** versus **processing aid**. Processing demands relate to the amount of cognitive effort required to understand a given story, whereas processing aids serve to facilitate story comprehension. Each of the components listed in Table 3.1 can function as either a processing aid or processing demand in a story.

In creating Tailored Stories, the goal is to balance the story components so that each story contains mostly elements that the child can easily process (e.g., familiar vocabulary and syntax, concrete ideas), with only one or two challenging story elements, chosen to address the child's goals. (See the Tailored Stories formula on page 74.) With the story components balanced in this way, the child should, in theory, be able to devote most of his mental resources to processing the challenging material as well as the story as a whole.

29

Elements of Cognitive Complexity

Event Knowledge

TAILORED STORY COMPONENTS					
Elements of Cognitive Complexity			Elements of Linguistic Complexity		
Event Knowledge	Contextualization	Story Memory	Story Text	Syntax	Semantics

"A narrative is more than just a piece of connected discourse; it is an account of an event. In order to produce a narrative, one must have knowledge about the event that is the topic of the narrative."

Hudson & Shapiro (1991, p. 90)

Scripts to Stories

The research of Nelson and Gruendel (1986) and others has taught us that young children organize their understanding of the world in the context of familiar events and routines. As they begin to recognize patterns in their experiences, children create scripts, or mental representations of the repeated events in their lives.

Young children often reveal early event knowledge by demonstrating anticipation of an upcoming action in a familiar routine. For example, a child may crawl toward the high chair upon seeing that Mommy is preparing food, or extend a foot when Daddy holds up a sock. Once playing peek-a-boo starts to become an internalized routine, the child often starts to squeal in anticipation of what is to come when a parent covers his or her face with a blanket.

As they progress, young children demonstrate knowledge of familiar events and routines by performing sequences of related actions without assistance. For example, a child might climb the ladder of a slide, sit at the top, and push off to slide down, or he may take a DVD out of its case, insert it in the DVD player, and press the "play" button. In time, children will act out their mental scripts for familiar events in pretend play, as in covering a doll with a blanket and saying "night-night."

The content of a child's event knowledge comes to provide the foundation for stories. According to Engel (1999),

> Nelson's theory emphasizes the idea that the world is experienced in socially
> meaningful units – event sequences – rather than as a set of perceptually

based abstractions (blue things, round things, square things). ... This model of how children make sense of experience, the script, looks a lot like a story, an event with actions, actors, and objects, occurring in time and space. This is no accident; scripts are narratives in germ. (p. 31)

Event Knowledge and Children with CLP

"It is not clear how much experience with a given event a child needs to form a script for that event. Normally developing children probably begin to script on the basis of a single encounter with an event. It is possible that some language/learning impaired children may require more experiences, or even some overt external help with structuring the experience, to know what the key or main elements are."

Naremore, Densmore, & Harmon (1995, p. 121)

There are many reasons why children with CLP may not acquire event knowledge in the same ways as their typically developing peers. Some children are less likely to recognize patterns in experience or create mental representations of their experiences due to cognitive limitations. Children with ASD may have a limited bank of event knowledge because they tend to observe the actions of others less and participate less often in socially based events in their lives than many other children. Further, children with language impairments may have incomplete comprehension and memory of events due to problems understanding the language associated with them. These issues and others can hinder the acquisition of event knowledge.

As a group, children with CLP differ widely in terms of their internalized event scripts. A child with severe cognitive impairments may have difficulty forming mental representations for even simple, familiar events such as bath time; however, the same child might know the steps involved in preparing a bowl of cereal if that is an event that interests him. A somewhat less involved child might understand the concrete routines and events of her daily life but not have the ability to comprehend events she has never experienced. Slightly more advanced children begin to comprehend events they have observed but not experienced (e.g., cooking, driving, and shaving). And then as children develop more understanding of people and events in the world and the language to talk about them, they can begin to understand stories based on events completely outside of their experience such as a space war or a prince saving a princess from a dragon.

Event Knowledge as a Processing Aid

Relevant event knowledge aids comprehension and the retelling of a story. The opposite is also true. Without knowledge of the event on which a story is based, story comprehension is limited, especially for younger and lower functioning children.

> Research has shown that preschool children are able to recall stories, understand temporal sequences, and to draw inferences from text when the material they are thinking about refers to familiar events, but fail to display the same level when asked to remember or reason about unfamiliar situations. (Hudson, 2004, p. 127)

The truth of the above statement was clearly illustrated in one story-based therapy session with a boy named Jonathan. Jonathan, who was 11 years old at the time, had significant cognitive and language learning challenges, so the stories his SLP, Abby, used with him were based on routines and events that were familiar to him. One day Jonathan spied a set of deep-sea diver toys in Abby's cabinet. His eyes lit up, and he requested them by pointing and saying, "diver." Given his enthusiasm, Abby created a diving story with the toys. Jonathan stayed engaged and was able retell the story by himself after only a couple of attempts with low-level support.

Jonathan's mother later told Abby that her son liked to watch programs about diving on television. Until that time Abby had not thought Jonathan could relate to stories about events he had not directly experienced. Excited about the new realm of stories she might use in his narrative intervention, she pulled out the toys for a police-and-robber story, a favorite of many boys. She created a simple story that she thought was at an appropriate language level for Jonathan.

But Jonathan's initial interest in the story fizzled quickly, and he struggled more than usual with the story language. His mother reported that Jonathan had never been exposed to shows or stories with this type of theme. Since Jonathan had no knowledge of the event on which the police-robber story was based, the story was not a good vehicle for teaching him language.

Basing a story on an event for which a child already has a clear mental representation facilitates the comprehension process. One aspect of potential confusion or difficulty is removed. In this way, matching stories to the child's event knowledge serves as a processing aid.

Event Knowledge as a Learning Target

Event knowledge, like each of the Tailored Story Components, can be used on either side of the processing equation – as a learning aid or a learning target. As noted earlier, basing a story on an event or routine that is familiar to the child can facilitate the child's processing of the story. However, when a child has few event scripts or has incomplete scripts, there are times when a goal may focus on strengthening the child's event knowledge. In these cases, different story elements, such as decreased memory demands, contextualized visual cues, and familiar language, may be used to support attainment of the new learning material – event knowledge.

Event Knowledge Through the Nurturing Narratives Levels

The stages of early event knowledge are listed in the first column of Table 3.2. Examples of events upon which stories may be based at each stage appear in column two.

Table 3.2

Linking Stories to Event Knowledge

Stages of Early Event Knowledge	Event Examples
simple, familiar routines and events that the child frequently directly experiences	taking a bath; going to the playground
simple, familiar routines and events that the child has observed but *not* directly experienced	washing dishes; buying groceries
less frequent but directly experienced events	going to the doctor; buying new shoes
a broader array of events as long as the child demonstrates event knowledge for them	events associated with various occupations, such as firefighter or astronaut; fantasy themes like knights slaying monsters or super heroes demonstrating super powers

The complexity of story events evolves through the Nurturing Narratives Levels (see Chapter 4). Level I stories are based on simple events, whereas in Level II, problems and solutions are added to the story events. In Level III, further expansion includes increased reference to the relatively more abstract content of the characters' internal responses to the story events.

Children are naturally drawn to themes that interest them, so basing stories on a child's interests is strongly encouraged. A final note on event knowledge is the reminder that most children love humor and excitement. **Often the stories that tend to get the best responses are those that contain a funny or surprising element that the child can understand.**

Event Knowledge and the Two Types of Stories: Fictional Stories and Personal Narratives

Table 3.3 summarizes the role of event knowledge in different types of stories.

Table 3.3
Event Knowledge in Fictional Stories and Personal Narratives

Fictional Stories	Personal Narratives
Basing early stories on events for which the child has event knowledge facilitates story comprehension	Creating and telling stories based on personal experiences (events) helps build the child's autobiographical memories
Expansion of event knowledge can be targeted in later stories	Hearing others' personal narratives facilitates children's knowledge and memories of them in the events in their lives

Assessing Event Knowledge

Informal Assessment

It is especially important to obtain information about the event knowledge of lower functioning children, as their realm of event scripts, and hence the realm of events upon which stories can be meaningfully based, may be limited.

Naremore et al. (2001) suggest observing children in their natural environments. Participation in usual routines and in play can provide not only a window into the variety of event scripts a child has internalized, but also indications of how well developed and organized those scripts are. Additionally, children's chosen play activities can reveal what interests and motivates them.

Useful information regarding a child's interests and event knowledge may also be obtained from parents, teachers, aides, and others who are closely involved in the child's life. A checklist to help with assessing event knowledge is found in Appendix A.

Formal Assessment

The Story Completion subtest of the *Kaufman Assessment Battery for Children-II* (Kaufman & Kaufman, 2004) can provide information about a child's event knowledge. During this subtest, the child is shown a row of pictures that tell a story, but some of the pictures are missing. The child is given a set of pictures and places the missing picture/s in the correct location/s. Age range: 5 to 6.

Contextualization

TAILORED STORY COMPONENTS					
Elements of Cognitive Complexity			**Elements of Linguistic Complexity**		
Event Knowledge	Contextualization	Story Memory	Story Text	Syntax	Semantics

Contextualization – the second element of cognitive complexity – refers in part to "the degree to which the information referred to through language is physically present" (Norris & Hoffman, 1993, p. 41). A highly contextualized utterance might be "The boy is eating pizza." as a boy literally eats pizza. A slightly less contextualized scenario would be one in which a picture is shown of a boy eating pizza, or as a boy doll is manipulated to simulate eating a toy piece of pizza as the sentence is spoken. If another object like a paper triangle were substituted for the pizza, the utterance would be even less contextualized, and so on. **In Nurturing Narratives, contextualized visual cues are designed to help a child understand the story as it is told.**

Types of Contextualized Support

Visual Support – Toys and Props
Level I stories are made relatively concrete by acting them out with replicas and miniatures of people and objects as the stories are told. Later, in slightly less contextualized stories, substituted objects can be used; for example, a note card may be used to represent a doll's bed and a tissue may be used as a blanket.

Visual Support – Pictures
Realistic pictures that closely match the story text may also be used as contextualized support. Comprehension is facilitated if the pictures are not cluttered with unessential details. For example, looking at pictures for a story about a dog seeing, and then eating, the food in his bowl, one child got distracted by the dog's collar and missed the point of the story. The story picture would have been more effective if that unnecessary detail had been omitted.

In the beginning, a separate picture to depict the content of each sentence may be required for some children to understand the story. In time, more than one sentence can relate to a picture. Story pictures can be phased out when the child shows the ability to understand the story language without them.

Contextualization as a Processing Aid – Decontextualization as a Learning Target

In Nurturing Narratives, concrete contextualized language and visual cues are offered to facilitate story comprehension when a child needs them. Over time, aspects of the story presentation can become less contextualized as the child demonstrates increasing ability to think abstractly and create a mental representation of the story based on hearing or reading the story language without viewing visual representations.

Contextualization Through the Nurturing Narratives Levels

In Nurturing Narratives Level I, stories are generally told and retold in the present tense while the story is being acted out with toys or while the relevant pictures are viewed. In Level II, there is a progression toward decontextualization, until the child can tell the story independently in the past tense without visual support. Finally, in Level III, as more abstract words and concepts are introduced into stories for which objects and pictures cannot be used to explain their meanings, there is increasing reliance on language alone to make the story meaningful.

Level of Contextualized Support and the Two Types of Stories: Fictional Stories and Personal Narratives

Early fictional stories can be told with a higher level of contextualization in that they are told in the present tense with concrete language as they are acted out with realistic toy miniatures. Personal narratives are less contextualized by virtue of relating to past experiences; however, both types of stories can be told with a range of contextualized support that decreases with advancement through the levels, as illustrated in Table 3.4.

Table 3.4
Levels of Contextualization for Fictional Stories and Personal Narratives

Level of Contextualization	Fictional Stories	Personal Narratives
Higher	Early stories are told with concrete language while acted out with realistic props or toy miniatures or as clear, uncluttered pictures (one per sentence) are viewed	Early stories are told with concrete language and photos (usually one per sentence) The person telling the story is in every photo to facilitate autobiographical memory/memory of others for the child
Lower	- Pictures may become less explicit (e.g., simple sketches) and less closely match the story text - More abstract language is introduced - The story is retold with decreasing, and finally no, visual/verbal cues	

Assessing Need for Contextualized Support

Informal Assessment

To assess the need for contextualized support, vary the types of support and observe which conditions yield higher levels of engagement and comprehension. Some options are listed below.

- Acting out the story with toys versus telling it with pictures

- Acting out stories with realistic objects (e.g., toy miniatures) versus substituted objects (e.g., using a pencil to stand for a baseball bat)

- Using photographs versus drawings

- Presenting realistic drawings versus impressionistic sketches

- Presenting pictures that more, versus less, closely match the text

Formal Assessment

The *Preschool Language Assessment Instrument-Second Edition* (PLAI-2; Blank, Rose, & Berlin, 2003) assesses children's ability to comprehend different levels of abstraction in responding to items that involve matching, analysis, reordering, and reasoning.

Story Memory

TAILORED STORY COMPONENTS					
Elements of Cognitive Complexity			Elements of Linguistic Complexity		
Event Knowledge	Contextualization	Story Memory	Story Text	Syntax	Semantics

Story Memory and Children with CLP

Different issues affect how well a child can remember a story. Certainly, understanding of the story is a major factor. In other sections of this chapter, discussion focuses on the importance of basing stories on events the child understands, providing contextualized clues to meaning, and shaping the linguistic features of stories to facilitate story comprehension.

Other factors that influence a child's story memory include how long and complicated the story is and whether or not the child has an internalized "story template." Having a mental framework for stories aids story comprehension and memory; however, children with CLP often have difficulty gleaning the pattern of stories.

One way this issue is addressed in Nurturing Narratives is by starting with the simplest story template and providing the child repeated exposure to stories written in that format. In time, many children begin to show indications of having a sense that stories start with an introduction of characters, followed by actions and the characters' feeling about the action. Then experience with stories in which additional story features are systematically added can help a child expand his internalized story framework.

Controlling Memory Demands as a Processing Aid

Controlling the length and complexity of stories are two ways we can influence children's memory of stories. As the child demonstrates readiness for greater memory demands, stories can be systematically lengthened and expanded as in the following example.

The earliest stories, referred to as "bare-bones stories," typically contain only **a character, an action, and a feeling.**

Here is a boy. He is swimming. He is happy!

Once the child has mastered retelling bare-bones stories, stories can be systematically lengthened. In the following version, **setting information** was added to the bare-bones story above.

This is a boy. He is in the ocean. He is swimming. The boy is having fun!

The story may be further lengthened by including a **story surprise or problem**.

This is a boy. He is swimming in the ocean.
Oh no! Here is a shark! The boy is afraid!

Story length and complexity can also be expanded to include a **resolution to the problem** and a **change in feeling**.

The boy is swimming. Oh no! Here is a shark! The boy is afraid!
He is climbing in the boat. Now the shark cannot bite him.
The boy is happy/relieved!

Story Memory as a Learning Target

One goal in Nurturing Narratives is for children to be able to hold stories in memory and retell them independently. Limiting the level of processing demand of other elements of story complexity supports attainment of this goal. So does use of scaffolds, such as visual memory cues and verbal prompts, which are gradually faded as the story is repeatedly practiced.

Progression of Story Memory Demands Through the Nurturing Narratives Levels

Early stories are three to four sentences long and gradually increase in length. Once the child demonstrates evidence of beginning to form a mental template for these bare-bones stories, the framework of stories is systematically expanded.

Early stories are retold jointly with visual cues present. In Level II, the child begins to retell stories from memory after a period of supported practice. In Level III, independent retelling of stories is encouraged after fewer rounds of supported practice

Table 3.5 demonstrates the progression from a high level of support and a low level of demand for the child's story memory to higher levels of expectation for the child to remember the story with decreasing levels of visual and verbal cueing. The similarities and differences in the ways story memory is facilitated during the telling of fictional stories and personal narratives are also summarized.

Table 3.5

Story Memory and the Two Types of Stories: Fictional Stories and Personal Narratives

	Fictional Stories	**Personal Narratives**
High Level of Memory Support	• Story length and complexity are controlled – initially 3-4 simple sentences • Stories are repeatedly practiced and jointly retold with visual & verbal support	
	Stories are told and practiced in different ways (e.g., with toys, pictures, or written text while role-playing, imitating, or completing sentences). Maximum support is offered as needed during story retelling.	Using photos, a "conversation facilitator" helps the child recall a personal experience and then create and practice telling a story about the experience. Later the conversation facilitator aids the child in retelling the story to another person. Maximum support is offered.
Increased Memory Demands	The child is asked to retell stories: (a) of increasing length and complexity, (b) with decreased scaffolding, (c) with fewer practice trials, and (d) independently without visual/verbal support.	

Assessing Story Memory

Informal Assessment

1. Story memory may be assessed by observing how the child responds when the story length (number of sentences) is systematically increased and elements of complexity (e.g., setting, story problem) are gradually added.

2. During child observation or parent/caregiver interview, determine whether the child:

    - makes references to the past

    - reenacts familiar events or themes

Formal Assessment

During administration of the *Renfrew Language Scales Bus Story Test* (Renfrew, 1997), the child is told a story and then asked to retell it while viewing the story pictures. The child's ability to remember details in the story is measured in the "Information" score. Age range: 3-8 years.

Elements of Linguistic Complexity

Story Text

TAILORED STORY COMPONENTS					
Elements of Cognitive Complexity			**Elements of Linguistic Complexity**		
Event Knowledge	Contextualization	Story Memory	Story Text • "bare-bones" • elaborated text • unaltered text	Syntax	Semantics

Story Text and Children with CLP

Story texts are comprised of multiple related sentences. This feature in itself can pose a processing challenge for some children with CLP. Furthermore, most published children's stories are written in a manner that requires children to relate their background knowledge to the text and make inferences regarding the characters' thoughts and actions in order to really understand the story.

Tailored Story Components

Let's refer to a popular preschool level story, *Mrs. Wishy-Washy*, for an example. *Mrs. Wishy-Washy,* by Joy Cowley, is a delightful story about some farm animals who like to play in the mud, and their owner who wants the animals to be clean. Mrs. Wishy-Washy bathes each animal; yet, just as soon as she has washed them all and turned her back, the animals race off to play in the mud again.

The text of this story contains several inferences. For example, the story never states that the pig likes the mud; rather the text reads "Oh lovely mud, said the pig, and he rolled in it." Similarly, Mrs. Wishy-Washy's dislike of the animals' unclean state is only indirectly conveyed in the line, "Just look at you! she screamed." The pictures do support comprehension of the text, however; the animals are smiling as they play in the mud, and Mrs. Wishy-Washy looks dismayed when she sees the dirty animals. Yet, even so, to understand these lines in the story, children need to tap their knowledge of women and animals on the subject of cleanliness, and must understand that different characters can have differing perspectives and desires which will influence their actions.

From a young age, children typically are actively making "Aha!"-inferred connections and predictions as they listen to stories. This is one of the reasons they find stories so engaging. However, for many children with CLP, this level of processing is too challenging. Quite often their mental effort is expended during the lower level processing of the words, sentences, and stated information in the story, leaving no resources left for the job of deciphering inferred information.

Story Text as a Processing Aid

Two styles of text, "bare-bones" and "elaborated text," are commonly used as scaffolds in Nurturing Narratives to aid story processing. Typically developing children tend to find stories written in these styles uninteresting because all the information is clearly stated, often redundantly, thereby eliminating the need for analyzing and hypothesizing. But these styles of text are often a key element in making stories comprehensible for children with CLP.

Bare-Bones Text

Bare-bones stories contain the simplest sentence patterns and include only concrete vocabulary that the child already knows. The stories are very short – three to four sentences – so the child has less to synthesize to process the story as a whole. Having fewer sentences also reduces demands on memory when the story is recalled and retold.

Bare-bones stories are comprised of the most elementary story components – character and action. They end with a "feeling" (He is happy.) or "coda" (It is fun!), which provides a consequence to the action and ties the story together. The inclusion of emotion words beginning in the earliest stories helps to highlight for the child the importance of paying attention to people's emotions and mental states. It also fosters an understanding of the causal relationship between events and people's/characters' internal reactions.

If one wanted to revise a portion of the Mrs. *Wishy-Washy* story to create a bare-bones story, it could go like this …

> *The pig is dirty. The lady is washing the pig.*
> *Now the pig is clean. The lady is happy.*

Repeated exposure to bare-bones stories can facilitate internalization of a simple story framework, and such mental frameworks for stories can in turn facilitate comprehension, memory, and creation of stories.

Use of Bare-Bones Stories to Improve Communicative Interactions and Early Narrative Skills

Emilio, a 14-year-old boy with autism and cognitive impairment, was one child who benefited from extended experience with bare-bones stories. Emilio could produce simple sentence patterns, and at times approached others with the seeming intent to tell them about something of interest to him. However, he typically initiated communication with a single noun or verb and then looked at his listener expectantly. The communication partner, pleased that the child wanted to communicate but failing to understand the message, would then start to ask questions to try to piece together what Emilio really wanted to say. This usually took a bit of work that sometimes ended with Emilio's thought being successfully conveyed. But often it did not.

For several months, Emilio's narrative intervention involved short, simple stories that had the bare-bones framework of character-action-feeling and contained vocabulary and sentence patterns that he understood. The stories were practiced until Emilio could retell them on his own.

For a long time, Emilio retold stories in the exact words in which they were told to him. He was relying on his good rote memory skills rather than tapping his language knowledge. However, in time, he began to use some of his own wording while retaining the meaning of the story as he retold stories.

Emilio has now had lots of practice retelling simple stories to a level of fluency and, with prompting, is sharing those stories with other people in his life. He has progressed to the point where he generally begins spontaneous communication with an indication of who the character in the story is, and sometimes provides information about the action in the story. These are considered indications that Emilio is beginning to internalize the simple story framework. A listener may still need to probe to get clearer information, but the process is less laborious and more enjoyable for both Emilio and the other person. Emilio is initiating communication with others much more frequently.

It is thought that using stories that contained vocabulary and syntax that Emilio already understood and exposing him to several such stories that followed a simple story framework worked synergistically to assist him in understanding the stories as whole entities, helped him retell the stories in social situations with less difficulty, and facilitated his recognition and internalization of the form of simple stories.

For many children, story-based intervention is initiated with bare-bones stories. The SLP sees if this level of story is easy or poses challenges for the child. If the child is able to handle it without difficulty, other elements of complexity can be systematically added into the stories until an appropriate level of challenge is determined.

Elaborated Text

Elaborated text is a style of writing stories that consists of the following features:

- concepts in the story are clearly connected

- new words and ideas are defined or described

- answers to questions the child will be asked are embedded

- the need for inferencing, or reading between the lines, is reduced

Elaborated texts, being relatively wordy, do not lend themselves to rote memorization (as bare-bones stories might), and thereby can compel the child to focus on comprehending the story to aid his ability to retell it. The ultimate goal is for children to have an integrated understanding of the stories and the expressive language skills to be able to adequately retell them in their own words. The use of elaborated text is intended, in part, to facilitate attainment of that goal.

Using Elaborated Text to Connect Story Ideas and Simplify Inferences

Children with CLP who are still struggling to understand single sentences often have difficulty comprehending the relationship between the sentences in a story, especially if that relationship is not stated explicitly. For example, if one of these children heard the sentences, "The baby is crying. Mom is getting a bottle. She is feeding the baby. Now the baby is happy," he might not recognize how these ideas are related. As this text is written, a child would have to infer why the baby was crying, why Mom fed her, and why the baby was then happy. An elaborated version that would reduce the need for inferencing might be, "The baby is crying because she is hungry. Mom knows the baby wants to eat. Mom is feeding the baby. Now the baby is not hungry so she feels happy."

In Table 3.6 we see how a segment of *Mrs. Wishy-Washy* might be rewritten using elaborated text to reduce the need for inferencing.

Table 3.6

Passage from* Mrs. Wishy-Washy *Rewritten with Elaborated Text

Excerpt from the original text of *Mrs. Wishy-Washy*	Excerpt from original text of *Mrs. Wishy-Washy* rewritten with elaborated text
"Oh lovely mud," said the pig,	Here is a pig. He sees some mud. Pigs like to play in mud. This pig wants to roll in the mud.
and he rolled in it …	The pig is happy because he is rolling in the mud.
Along came Mrs. Wishy-Washy.	Uh oh, here comes Mrs. Wishy-Washy.
"Just look at you!" she screamed.	She is looking at the muddy pig, and she is not happy. She wants the pig to be clean, but he is dirty!
"In the tub you go"…	Mrs. Wishy-Washy is thinking she can give the pig a bath. She says "Pig, get in the bathtub."
In went the pig, wishy-washy, wishy-washy."	The pig climbs in the bathtub and Mrs. Wishy-Washy washes him.

Note that the syntax in the elaborated versions of the hungry baby and dirty pig stories is more advanced than in the original versions of these stories. The challenge of using elaborated text as a scaffold for comprehension is to clarify ideas for the child *while* keeping the language at a meaningful and manageable level. During the progression through the Nurturing Narratives Levels, suggestions are offered for how to maintain this balance.

Using Elaborated Text to Define New Vocabulary

When children with CLP hear a new word in a story, they are less likely than their neurotypical peers to be able to infer its meaning (from what else has been said) and continue to follow the thread of the story. It is possible that they will disregard the word or get distracted wondering what the word means. Either way, comprehension of the story as a whole will probably be undermined. This effect gets multiplied when stories contain several unfamiliar words.

Words that are anticipated to be challenging for the child can be defined right in the context of the story using elaborated language. Embedding description of unfamiliar words in the story text can function to help the child relate new with existing vocabulary knowledge as in the following excerpt.

> Melissa ran out into the pouring rain and got really wet. When Mom saw her, she said, "You are *drenched*!" Melissa was *drenched*! Her hair, her clothes, her shoes and socks, and her whole body were completely wet and dripping with water. The only times Melissa had been this wet before were when she was in the bathtub or a swimming pool.

Progression of Story Text Through the Nurturing Narratives Levels

The earliest Nurturing Narratives stories have bare-bones texts; then stories begin to be written with elaborated texts to aid story comprehension. Later, elaborated language is used more sparingly, only as needed. The end goal (for some children) is to be able to use unaltered children's story texts and rely on discussion alone to address comprehension difficulties when they arise.

Story Text: Personal Narratives and Fictional Stories

The earliest versions of both types of stories contain bare-bones texts. Elaborated language is used in later stories as needed to facilitate comprehension.

Assessing Story Text Needs

Informal Assessment

A child's need for revised text can be ascertained while observing how he comprehends stories told with and without text adaptations (e.g. bare-bones or elaborated texts). Levels of elaborated text range from explicit text (which connects all ideas, reduces the need for inferencing as much as possible, and defines any challenging words) to texts in which some information is only implied and, therefore, requires inferencing.

Syntax

TAILORED STORY COMPONENTS					
Elements of Cognitive Complexity			Elements of Linguistic Complexity		
Event Knowledge	Contextualization	Story Memory	Story Text	Syntax • sentence patterns • phrase elaboration • verb tense	Semantics

In general, structural aspects of language are introduced into Nurturing Narratives stories in the order in which they are acquired in typical child development. Addition of the various grammatical morphemes in stories is usually left to the discretion of the SLP. However, it is recommended that some language forms be included due to the integral role they play in important narrative skills. These forms include certain sentence patterns, early phrase elaborations, and verb tenses.

Sentence Patterns Through the Nurturing Narratives Levels

Level I: The earliest Level I stories contain only the following simple sentence patterns. The first two are needed to introduce the most fundamental components of stories – characters and actions. The third pattern supports ending the story with a feeling or coda.

1. Subject-Verb (e.g., *The boy is swimming. The girls are dancing.*)

2. Subject-Verb-Object (e.g., *Here is a boy. The boy is eating ice cream.*)

3. Subject-Verb-Complement (e.g., *They are sad. It is fun!*)

The Subject-Verb-Verb (SVV) sentence pattern is usually introduced in late Level I. This sentence form is highlighted because it lends itself to expressing story characters' desires, preferences, and needs (e.g., *She wants to eat. He likes to swing*). The SVV sentence pattern also supports two other linguistic structures: the future tense (e.g., *Dora is going to climb.*) and the expression of possibility (e.g., *The lady can swim.*).

Level II: Compound and complex sentences tie ideas together and express how they are related. In late Level II, compound sentences, with clauses joined by *and*, *but*, and *so* begin to be included in stories. At the same time, complex sentences in which two clauses are linked by the conjunction *because* are also introduced. Sentence forms containing *because* and *so* are important due to their role in spotlighting causal relationships as stories begin to contain problems, solutions, and characters' reactions.

Level III: In Level III, stories begin to contain more complex sentences. Three complex sentence forms are emphasized in particular. The first two are sentence forms that express temporal and causal relationships (e.g., "The girl ate a snack before she went to basketball practice." "Since the bus already left, he walked to school.").

The third complex sentence form featured at this time is that which contains a *sentential complement*. This sentence form is important because the only verbs that may be used in it are verbs of communication and mental state verbs. It is also significant because it is the sentence form used to express "false belief" statements. Sentences containing mental state verbs and false-belief statements are used to convey information about story characters' perspectives.

Examples of sentences containing a verb of communication and a mental state verb followed by a sentential complement (underlined) might be "Dad *said* he is going to wash the car." and "She *thought* her dog was in the yard.," respectively. In both of these sentences, the information in the sentential complement could be false while each sentence as a whole is true. Children need to understand such sentences in order to comprehend false-belief statements and vice versa. They also need to use this sentence form to talk about false-beliefs. This area is of particular difficulty for children with ASD.

Early Phrase Elaboration

Starting in late Level I, phrases begin to be elaborated in order to clarify certain information in the story. For example, a **preposition** may be used to state the setting of the story (e.g., "at the park"), or the whereabouts of a character (e.g., "in the pool") or an object (e.g., "in the box."). Prepositions are also needed to express the early perspective-taking concept, "looking = wanting" (e.g., "The girl is looking at the jungle gym. She wants to climb."). Finally, **Adjectives** and **adverbs** may be used to clarify nouns and verbs (e.g., "Dad can fix the *broken* truck." "The car is going *fast*.").

Particularly in early stories, phrases are elaborated only as needed; inclusion of only critical information serves as a processing aid for children who have difficulty determining which information is important for understanding the story. In the last example, for instance, the sentence would simply read "The car is going." unless the car going *fast* was significant in the story.

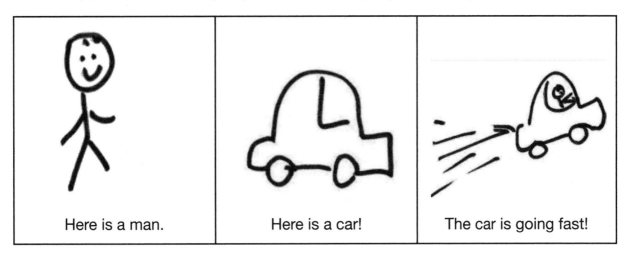

| Here is a man. | Here is a car! | The car is going fast! |

Verb Tense

Many children with CLP struggle with the complexities of verb tense. Some children have a difficult time understanding the abstract concept of present, past, and future. Others understand the concept but get confused by the singular and plural forms of verbs (*he eats, they eat*), the three different ending sounds of regular past tense verbs (*walked, played, batted*), and the various irregular past tense verbs (*ate, slept, ran*).

Difficulties with verb tense can significantly hinder fluent story retelling. When this type of difficulty is observed, we often make most of the verbs in the story progressive tense verbs because doing so simplifies the verb tense issue significantly. Consider the comparisons in Table 3.7 involving the irregular verb *to run*.

Table 3.7
Comparison of Simple and Progressive Tense

	Simple Tense	Progressive Tense
Singular present	runs	is running
Plural present	run	are running
Singular past	ran	was running
Plural past	ran	were running
Singular future	will run	is going to run
Plural future	will run	are going to run

When the progressive tense is used, the child only needs to learn the auxiliary forms – *is*, *are*, *was*, and *were* – and follow them with the *-ing* form of the verb (e.g., *eating*) to express almost any present or past tense verb.

The future progressive tense simply involves adding "going to + verb" to the present auxiliary forms *is* and *are* (e.g., *is/are going to eat*). The following story illustrates how the progressive tense was used when teaching one child to retell stories in the past tense.

Use of Progressive Tense in Teaching Children to Retell a Story in the Past Tense

In Marco's language therapy sessions, his SLP, Joan, had been working with him on retelling simple stories in the present tense while the stories were acted out with toys or as Marco viewed the story pictures. Most of the stories' verbs were in the present progressive tense.

When Marco met the goal of being able to "fluently retell simple stories with visual cues present," Joan decided it was time to address Marco's next goal, which involved retelling simple stories in the past tense. Joan began with the following story:

> *Here is a boy. Here is a slide. The boy is climbing.*
>
> *The boy is sliding. It is fun!*

When Marco easily retold the story in the present tense, Joan removed the story toys from the table and told the story in the past tense, again using mostly progressive tense verbs. Joan gestured toward where the objects and actions had been on the table as she mentioned them.

> *There **was** a boy. There **was** a slide. The boy **was** climbing.*
>
> *The boy **was** sliding. It **was** fun!*

Joan then asked Marco if he could "tell the story with no toys." When Marco used a present tense verb in the first sentence, Joan playfully said, "Here **IS** a boy?? (as she gestured toward the table). There **WAS** a boy." When Marco said, "The boy is sliding." Joan said, "The boy **IS** sliding?? No, the boy is not here now. The boy **WAS** sliding."

Joan exposed Marco to several stories presented in the same way. She started with a simple story told in the present progressive tense with visual cues (toys or pictures) in view, then scaffolded retelling of the story in past progressive tense without visual cues. She also used consistent verbal cueing. In time, Marco began to understand the concept of *present* and *past*, and began retelling stories in past tense given less and less scaffolding.

In the example above, Joan simplified the task, in part, by using progressive tense verbs. It was easier for Marco to understand the distinction between *is sliding* and *was sliding*, for example, than had Joan used *slides* and *slid*.

Using progressive tense verbs in early stories can be a powerful therapy tool. Many children, like Marco, are able to retell stories much more easily when the stories are primarily in the progressive tense. Sometimes the present progressive tense wording sounds a little off, but if using it means the difference between the message being communicated or not, or the delivery being less or more labored, the trade-off is worth it. Nevertheless, the progressive tense is not used for all verbs. In fact, the simple present tense is always used for a specific handful of verbs. These include forms of *to be, to have, to see, to like* and *to want*, as the progressive forms of these verbs usually sound particularly awkward (e.g., *is being, is liking*). Telling stories in predominantly progressive tense can be phased out when the child no longer needs it to keep the stories manageable.

Progression of Syntax Through the Nurturing Narratives Levels

Table 3.8 summarizes the progression and roles of the syntactic forms targeted in stories through the Nurturing Narratives Levels

Table 3.8

Progression of Syntax Through the Nurturing Narratives Levels

Level	Form	Purpose
Early Level I	Sentence pattern: Subject-Verb Sentence pattern: Subject-Verb-Object	Introduce basic story components: "characters" and "actions"
	Sentence pattern: Subject-Verb-Complement	Express characters' feelings; express consequence of action
	Mostly present progressive tense	Simplify verb tense
Late Level I	Sentence pattern: Subject-Verb-Verb	Support use of early mental state verbs; talk about future and possibility
	Prepositional phrases	State "setting"
Level II	Past tense verbs	Talk about the past
	Compound sentences with *and, but,* and *so*	Join/relate clauses/ideas; express causality
	Complex sentence with *because*	Express causality
Level III	Complex sentences with time words (e.g., *while, before, after*)	Express temporal relationships
	Sentences that contain sentential complements	Support use of verbs of communication, higher level mental state verbs, and expression of "false belief"
	Other complex sentence forms	Express relationships between ideas

---

Assessing Morphology and Syntax

Numerous tools are available for assessing a child's morphology and syntax skills at the preschool level, including language sample analysis; *Structured Photographic Expressive Language Test-Preschool 2 – SPELT-P 2* (Dawson, Stout, & Eyer, 2003), age range: 3 to 5 years, 11 months; *Clinical Evaluation of Language Fundamentals-Preschool, 2nd Edition* (CELF Preschool 2), selected subtests (Wiig, Secord, & Semel, 2004), age range: 3-6; *Test of Language Development-Primary, 4th Edition* (TOLD-P:4), selected subtests (Newcomer & Hammill, 2008), age range: 4 to 8 years, 11 months; *Diagnostic Evaluation of Language Variation (DELV)-Norm Referenced*, selected subtests (Seymour, Roeper, & de Villiers, 2005), age range: 4-9 years; and others.

Semantics

TAILORED STORY COMPONENTS					
Elements of Cognitive Complexity			**Elements of Linguistic Complexity**		
Event Knowledge	Contextualization	Story Memory	Story Text	Syntax	Semantics • concrete to abstract vocabulary • theory of mind • inferencing

Concrete to Abstract Vocabulary

We talk about word meanings as ranging from concrete to abstract. The meanings of concrete words can be taught by referencing observable objects and actions. Examples include, *ball, Mommy, dog, eat, sit,* and *run*. Concrete words are the easiest to teach and learn.

On the concrete-to-abstract continuum, the next category of words is referred to as being "perceptually-verbally explainable" (term adapted from Blank, Marquis, & Klimovitch,1995). The meanings of these words can be partly understood on the basis of physical referents, but not completely. Verbal explanation is required to convey the other parts of their meanings. An example of a perceptually-verbally explainable word would be the noun *race*. Part of its meaning can be observed in the act of running, but other aspects need to be described with language in order for the full meaning of the word to be understood.

The most abstract words are "verbally-explainable." That is, their meanings can only be conveyed through verbal definition and require reasoning to understand. A word like *competitive* would fall in this category.

Concrete	**Perceptually-Verbally Explainable**	**Verbally Explainable**
Run	*Race*	*Competitive*

The Nurturing Narratives earliest stories primarily contain concrete nouns and verbs that are already in the child's repertoire. This is particularly true when stories are first introduced into the child's intervention program. When children are ready for new vocabulary words to be introduced in early stories, the words should have meanings which can be concretely demonstrated. Table 3.11 (on page 60) outlines the progression of semantics through the Nurturing Narratives Levels.

Assessing Vocabulary Knowledge

A variety of instruments may be used to assess early vocabulary knowledge, including *MacArthur-Bates Communicative Development Inventories (CDI), Second Edition* (Fenson, Marchman, Thal, Dale, Reznick, & Bates, 2007), age range: 8-37 months; *Peabody Picture Vocabulary Test, Fourth Edition* (PPVT-4; Dunn & Dunn, 2007), age range: 2 years, 6 months-90+ years; *Montgomery Assessment of Vocabulary Acquisition* (MAVA; Montgomery, 2008), age range: 3 years, 0 months-12 years, 11 months.

Theory of Mind

Theory of mind (ToM) involves understanding another's thoughts and feelings and underpins the ability to explain and predict the behavior of other people. ToM skills are crucial for developing social relationships and for understanding stories.

Early ToM skills develop on a continuum. They begin in infancy with sharing joint attention and culminate in the preschool years with comprehension of false beliefs (Astington, 2001). The latter skill entails understanding that someone else wrongly thinks something is true based on his or her perspective/current knowledge while knowing – based on one's own perspective/knowledge – that that belief is false. Understanding another's false belief requires holding both one's own and another's belief in mind at the same time. Attainment of this ability is considered to mark a critical turning point in the development of perspective-taking skills.

Bruner (1987) spoke of stories as having two main components, which he called the "landscape of action" and the "landscape of consciousness." The **landscape of action** relates to the series of actions in the story, whereas the **landscape of consciousness** refers to "what those in the action know, think or feel, or do not know, think or feel" (p. 14).

The landscape of consciousness is an important part of stories, even in stories for very young children. Based on a review of 317 books for preschool-aged children, Westby and Wilson (2005) reported that 78% contained references to internal states, 34% contained a false belief, and 31% contained deception (slide 21). The authors noted that in order to understand such references, children need such ToM skills as:

- being aware of what other people are thinking

- predicting what others are thinking from what we know about them and the world

- using what we know about other people to understand a situation (slide 18)

Theory of Mind Skills and Children with CLP

Children with CLP often demonstrate problems with ToM skills. Although as a group they demonstrate a range of ability, children with ASD characteristically have difficulty with perspective taking (Baron-Cohen, 1995). Other children with CLP may understand that other people have thoughts that are different from their own but are unable to infer what story characters are thinking and feeling if that information is only alluded to in the text. And even if they can comprehend and infer others' perspectives, many children with CLP have working memory problems that make it hard for them to hold these perspectives in mind while they are thinking about and/or doing something else like trying to process the language forms in a story.

Two recent studies indicated that children with language impairment (LI) have difficulty making social inferences in stories (Ford & Milosky, 2003; Spackman, Fujiki, & Brinton, 2006). In both studies, children were read simple three-sentence stories accompanied by story pictures and were asked to predict how the character would feel about what had happened in the story. (The pictures and text of one story from Ford & Milosky [2003] may be found in Figure 3.1.) Compared to age-matched typically developing peers, both younger and older children with LI (ages 5-12) had difficulty with this task. As the authors of these studies point out, this type of difficulty has negative implications for children with LI in real-life social situations as well as with story comprehension.

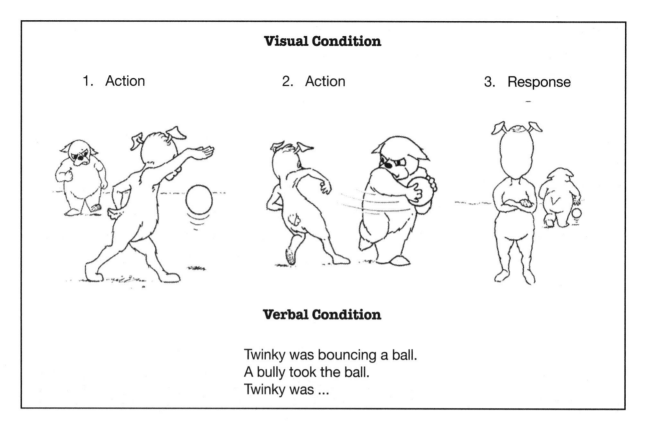

Visual Condition

1. Action   2. Action   3. Response

Verbal Condition

Twinky was bouncing a ball.
A bully took the ball.
Twinky was ...

Figure 3.1. **Sample of social inferencing.**

From "Inferring emotional reactions in social situations: Differences in children with language impairment" by J. A. Ford and L. M. Milosky. *Journal of Speech, Language, and Hearing Research, 46,* 21-30. Copyright 2003 by American Speech-Language-Hearing Association. Reprinted with permission.

Progression of Theory of Mind Through the Nurturing Narratives Levels

Words that refer to people's internal states are abstract and, for the most part, are only verbally explainable. Yet, because it is necessary to understand ToM concepts to be able to comprehend almost all stories, ToM concepts and vocabulary are included in all levels of Nurturing Narratives stories.

The earliest stories include reference to characters' simple emotions. Then stories begin to contain early mental state verbs, which express basic preferences, desires, and needs of the characters. The vocabulary used to express these concepts includes the emotions words *happy*, *sad*, *mad*, and *scared/afraid,* and the early mental state verbs *want(s)*, *want(s) to*, *like(s)*, *like(s) to*, *need(s)*, and *need(s) to*.

Story excerpts containing basic emotion words:

The dog is barking. The baby feels *scared*.

The ice cream fell. Andy is *sad*.

Tailored Story Components

Story excerpts containing early mental state verbs:

Dora sees the tree. She *wants* to climb.

Rob is drinking juice. He *likes* juice.

Nancy has some soup. She *needs* a spoon.

Higher level mental state verbs such as *think, know, guess, remember, forget, hope, realize, understand,* and *wonder* may be included in stories when the child demonstrates the ability to understand them. Emphasis is placed on understanding, and later inferring and explaining, story characters' mental states, intentions, and motivations. In addressing ToM skills in story-based activities, the intent is to foster social comprehension in interpersonal situations as well as facilitate story comprehension. Table 3.9 summarizes the ToM skills that are targeted in each of the Nurturing Narratives Levels.

Table 3.9
Theory of Mind Through the Nurturing Narratives Levels

Level	Theory of Mind Skills
Level I	Identify and name simple emotions Identify and express simple intentions, preferences, and desires (e.g., *wants, wants to, likes, likes to, needs, needs to*)
Level II	Understand that certain stimuli and situations lead to certain mental states, which in turn prompt certain behaviors (e.g., lady sees mouse, feels scared, and runs away) Understand higher level mental states (e.g., *think, know, remember*) related to familiar events (e.g., Sally needs her shoes. She *knows* they are in the closet.)
Level III	Identify mental states Recognize that mental states can be inferred from situational cues Explain what others know and how they know it Make predictions about behavior based on mental states Understand and explain false beliefs

---

Assessing Early Theory of Mind Skills

Informal Assessment

1. In *Scaling of Theory of Mind Tasks*, Wellman and Liu (2004) reported on a study in which 75 children (ages 2 years, 11 months to 6 years, 6 months) were tested on seven tasks tapping different aspects of understanding persons' mental states. Results indicated a consistent progression in the children's ability to perform these tasks. The tasks are sufficiently described in the article to replicate.

2. The *Picture Sequencing Test* (Baron-Cohen, Leslie, & Frith, 1986) compared the performance of children with autism and Down Syndrome to that of typical preschoolers in sequencing story pictures and narrating descriptive, causal, and mental state stories. The study and the pictures are available from http://www.autismresearchcenter.com/tests/picturesequencing_test.asp.

3. *Teaching Children with Autism to Mind-Read: A Practical Guide for Teachers and Parents* (Howlin, Baron-Cohen, & Hadwin, 1999) provides pictures and tasks for assessing five levels of emotional understanding.

Formal Assessment

The NEPSY-II Theory of Mind subtest "assesses the ability to understand mental functions, the ability to understand that others have their own thoughts, ideas, and feelings, and the ability to understand how emotion relates to social context" (http://www.pearsonassessments.com/hai/images/Products/NEPSY-II/NEPSY-II_Test_Summary.pdf). This subtest is appropriate for ages 3-16.

Inferencing

Inferencing can be described in a variety of ways, including the following.

- One key way in which literal and inferential language uses are distinguished from each other relates to whether all of the needed information for comprehension is directly provided in the text or in pictures of a book or must be supplied in part by the listener's or reader's background knowledge or reasoning. (van Kleeck, Vander Woude, & Hammett, 2006, p. 86)

- The ability to make inferences is, in simple terms, the ability to use two or more pieces of information from a text in order to arrive at a third piece of information that is implicit. (Kispal, 2008, p. 6)

We often refer to inferencing as "reading between the lines." It involves assimilating the information given in the story text with one's own background knowledge to determine an implied, but not stated, meaning. It is necessary to understand inferred information in stories in order to comprehend them correctly.

Tailored Story Components

Children with CLP typically have difficulty with inferencing. They often have a paucity of background knowledge and/or do not understand that there is a meaning beyond what is explicitly stated in a story. Sometimes they rely too much on their personal knowledge and overlook important information in the story text (Buehl, 2001). Johnston (2006) reported, "Studies of narrative comprehension … have shown that children with SLI have difficulty answering questions about a story when inferences are required. … The immediate work of understanding the story facts may consume the available resources and leave children unable to integrate these meanings into a larger whole" (p. 56).

Reducing the Need for Inferencing to Aid Processing

Since inferencing is so challenging for children with CLP, a common practice in Nurturing Narratives is to reduce the need for inferencing in stories. Once children move beyond the need for bare-bones story texts, elaborated text is used as a comprehension scaffold to supply information that otherwise would only have been implied. Elaborated text is discussed in detail in the Story Text section of this chapter; however, here is an example of its use to reduce the need for inferencing.

The following excerpt from the story *Cat Traps* by M. Coxe (1996, pp. 5-9), is an example of a segment of text that provides little given information and requires considerable background information and inferencing ability to comprehend.

> Cat wants a snack.
>
> Cat sets a trap.
>
> Cat gets a bug.
>
> Ugh!

This story is rated by the publisher at the preschool/kindergarten level. Although it appears to be simple, there are a number of reasons why this passage from the story might not be meaningful to a child with CLP. For example, to understand this passage, a child must know that cats like to eat mice and don't like to eat bugs. The child needs to have event knowledge for "setting traps." The child must also be able to infer the causal connections between wanting a snack and setting a trap, between setting a trap and getting a bug, and between getting a bug and responding with disgust. Indeed, the processing requirements of this simple story segment are quite high.

Here is an elaborated version of the *Cat Traps* excerpt on the previous page:

> "Here is a cat. He is hungry. He wants to eat a snack. Cats like to eat mice but the cat does not have a mouse. He needs to catch one. The cat will use a trap to catch a mouse. A trap is a container for catching and holding animals. The cat knows that mice like to eat cheese. He puts some cheese in the trap. A mouse might go in the trap to eat the cheese. Then the cat could catch the mouse and eat it.
>
> Oh no! There is something in the trap but it is not a mouse. There is a bug in the trap! Ugh! Cats do not like to eat bugs. The cat is disappointed! He wanted to trap a mouse, but he trapped a bug."

As demonstrated, elaborated text can function as a processing aid or enhancer by helping to eliminate some of the story comprehension problems that children with CLP often experience. Telling the story with story toys (to include a trap if that word was unfamiliar) would also facilitate a child's comprehension of the ideas in this story.

Some children may always need help with the relatively complex process of inferencing; others will reach a point when they are ready for higher level story comprehension challenges. When this occurs, the development of their inferencing abilities can be facilitated, as discussed below.

Inferencing Skills as a Learning Target

According to Pelletier and Astington (2004), "It may be that children's understanding of actions precedes ability to consider the thoughts behind actions" (p. 8). It stands to reason that inferences based on observable actions are easier to grasp than inferences related to mental activity, such as desires and beliefs, which cannot be observed. Physical inferencing may prepare children for more abstract social inferencing. For this reason, it can be helpful to make a distinction between comprehension questions that require physical inferencing and those calling for social inferencing.

The story in Figure 3.1 contains examples of physical and social inferencing questions, which might be asked after presentation of the first story picture.

Here are two kids. They both want the doll! The girl and the boy are pulling on the doll.	The doll broke! The kids were pulling the doll's arms. They were pulling really hard and one of the doll's arms ripped off! The kids feel sad/sorry because they broke the doll.

Physical inference question:
 	
   What could/might happen to the doll?
 	
Social inference question:
 	
   How will the kids feel?	

Figure 3.2. Colorcard™ Sequencing – Cause and Effect series.

© Speechmark Ltd., 1997; www.speechmark.net. Pictures used with permission.

Table 3.10

Progression of Inferencing Through the Nurturing Narratives Levels

Level I	None
Level II	Reasoning about physical events
Level III	Reasoning about social situations and mental states

---

Assessing Inferencing Skills

Informal Assessment

During shared book reading, ask questions requiring causal explanations (e.g., "Why did the glass fall?" or "Why did the baby cry?") and/or predictive explanations (e.g., "What do you think the dog is going to do?").

Formal Assessment

The Preschool Language Assessment Instrument-Second Edition (PLAI-2; Blank et al., 2003) is a tool that assesses children's ability to comprehend different levels of abstraction in responding to items that involve matching, analysis, reordering, and reasoning.

Table 3.11 summarizes the progression and role of the semantic forms targeted in stories through the Nurturing Narratives Levels.

Table 3.11

Progression of Semantics Through the Nurturing Narratives Levels

Level	Vocabulary	Purpose
Early Level I	Mostly familiar, concrete nouns and verbs	Demonstrate meanings perceptually
	Basic emotions words – *happy, sad, mad, scared/afraid*	Facilitate early perspective taking
Late Level I	Early mental state verbs – *want(s), like(s), need(s)*	Facilitate early perspective taking
	Adverb *not*	Express negation
	Adverbs *now* and *then*	Express temporal relationships
	Modal *can*	Express potential or possibility
Level II	Increased range of emotion words	Facilitate perspective taking
	Verbs of communication (e.g., *said, yelled*)	Give characters voice
	Increased range of time words (e.g., *just then, first, soon, last*)	Express temporal relationships
	Some perceptually-verbally explainable words (e.g., *daughter, niece, wife*)	Expand understanding of more abstract words
	Conjunctions – *and, but, so, because*	Express relationships between ideas
Level II and III	Higher level mental state terms (e.g., *think, know, guess, remember, forget*)	Facilitate perspective taking
Level III	Time words – *before, after, when, while*	Express temporal relationships
	Conjunctions – *although, unless,* etc.	Express relationships between ideas
	Some words that are only "verbally-explainable"	Expand understanding of more abstract words

Balancing Processing Demands and Supports

In the beginning of this chapter, the idea of balancing the processing demands and processing supports in stories was introduced. Six elements of story complexity were described and discussed in terms of their role in stories as either a processing aid or a processing demand/ teaching target. Table 3.12 summarizes the elements of cognitive and linguistic complexity in each of these roles in stories.

Table 3.12

Elements of Cognitive and Linguistic Complexity in Tailored Stories

TAILORED STORIES	
Elements of Cognitive Complexity	**Elements of Linguistic Complexity**
Event Knowledge	Story Text Syntax
Event knowledge as a processing support: Base stories on familiar and/or simple events to facilitate story comprehension **Event knowledge as a learning target:** Lower other processing demands (e.g., use familiar vocabulary and syntax, decrease memory load) when facilitating expansion of existing event knowledge	**Story text as a processing support:** Use bare-bones text framework (character(s)-action(s)-feeling/coda) to facilitate comprehension of story as a whole, internalize a simple story framework, and highlight simple causal relations (e.g., story action and character's feeling) Use elaborated language to provide needed background information, define new words, and reduce the need for inferencing, thereby facilitating story comprehension **Story text as a learning target:** Use familiar story events, simplified language, visual supports, etc., to facilitate comprehension of inferences in non-elaborated texts

(continued on page 62)

61

TAILORED STORIES (cont.)	
Elements of Cognitive Complexity	**Elements of Linguistic Complexity**
Contextualization	**Syntax**
Contextualization as a processing support: Use story language that can be represented perceptually (acted out with toys, depicted in pictures, role-played) to facilitate comprehension of other story elements (e.g., new syntactic forms, vocabulary) and overall story comprehension **Decontextualization as a learning target:** Strengthen event knowledge, simplify language, shorten length of story, provide scaffolded story retelling practice, etc., to facilitate the ability to internalize the story and retell it without contextual cues Use elaborated language, visual supports, etc., to support comprehension of decontextualized language, "language for reporting, reasoning, predicting, and projecting into thoughts of others" (Westby & Wilson, 2005, slide 15)	Across a variety of studies, "children with SLI [specific language impairment], relative to age peers, consistently showed poorer comprehension of the complex sentences but not the simple sentences" (Montgomery, 2009, p. 281) **Syntax as a processing support:** Simplify syntax to facilitate comprehension of other story elements (e.g., new vocabulary or story as a complete entity) **Syntax as a learning target:** Lower other processing demands to facilitate comprehension and acquisition of new syntactic forms.
Memory	**Semantics**
Memory as a processing support: Limit length and complexity of story to facilitate comprehension of other story elements and the story as a whole **Memory as a learning target:** Lower other processing demands (e.g., base story on familiar events, use familiar vocabulary and syntax) when facilitating ability to remember longer stories	**Semantics as a processing support:** Use concrete vocabulary to facilitate processing of other story elements **Semantics as a learning target:** Lower complexity of other story elements and use contextualized cues, role-playing, and elaborated language to facilitate comprehension of more abstract vocabulary, ToM concepts, and inferences

Best practice involves use of evidence-based treatment strategies in speech and language intervention. Evidence-based support for the Tailored Story Components appears in Appendix F.

Chapter 4

The Nurturing Narratives Levels

Each Nurturing Narratives Level targets a range of story complexity for the Tailored Stories along with guidelines for narrative-based intervention. This chapter presents an overview of the Nurturing Narratives Levels. Chapter 5 focuses on guidelines for creating tailored personal narratives and fictional stories in each Level. Then, in Chapter 7, the three Levels are revisited with reference to story-based intervention.

NURTURING NARRATIVES LEVELS		
	Tailored Stories personal narratives and fictional stories	**Story Lessons** narrative-based intervention sessions
	Level of Story Complexity	**Primary Focus**
Level I Events	**Low** Simple stories are based on familiar events and routines or recent personal experiences	• Engagement, joint attention, and reciprocal interaction • Interactive retelling of simple stories • Automaticity of basic sentence patterns • Internalization of a simple story framework
Level II Surprises	**Moderate** Stories begin to contain problems and solutions	• Early conversation skills • Independent retelling of stories in past tense • Expression of temporal and causal relationships in stories
Level III Theory of Mind	**High** Stories focus on characters' thoughts and perspectives	• Independence in simple conversations • Theory of mind skills • Expanded repertoire of complex sentences

Level I – Events

NURTURING NARRATIVES LEVELS		
	Tailored Stories personal narratives and fictional stories	**Story Lessons** narrative-based intervention sessions
	Level of Story Complexity	**Primary Focus**
Level I Events	**Low** Simple stories are based on familiar events and routines or recent personal experiences	• Engagement, joint attention, and reciprocal interaction • Interactive retelling of simple stories • Automaticity of basic sentence patterns • Internalization of a simple story framework
Level II Surprises	**Moderate** Stories begin to contain problems and solutions	• Early conversation skills • Independent retelling of stories in past tense • Expression of temporal and causal relationships in stories
Level III Theory of Mind	**High** Stories focus on characters' thoughts & perspectives	• Independence in simple conversations • Theory of mind skills • Expanded repertoire of complex sentences

Children are ready for Level I when they (at least) demonstrate …

- response to bids for joint attention

- intentional communication

- event knowledge for familiar routines

- imitation of simple actions and words

- a small vocabulary of concrete nouns and verbs

Children in Level I often have significant developmental and learning challenges. These are children for whom engagement and meaningful and manageable learning content are most critical; hence, the level of story complexity is lowest.

Nurturing Narratives Levels

Since knowledge of the event on which a story is based facilitates both comprehension and retelling of stories, the earliest fictional stories are based on simple routines and events that are very familiar to the child. Personal narratives refer to recent, memorable experiences. The level of contextualization of Level I stories is high; fictional stories are told as they are acted out with toy miniatures or while the child views story pictures. Personal narratives are told with photographs. The stories are short (initially 3-4 sentences long), contain simple vocabulary and sentence patterns, and cover a short time span.

Level of Support/Demand: In general, children receive a high level of scaffolded support in Level I, while the level of demand for independent story retelling is low. Details of Level I story content are outlined in Table 4.1.

Table 4.1

Tailored Story Components: Level I

	Event Knowledge	Contextualization	Memory	Story Text	Syntax	Semantics
Early Level I Stories						
	• **Personal Narratives** are based on recent personal experiences • **Fictional Stories** are based on familiar routines and events the child has directly experienced	• **Personal Narratives:** photos (preferably) or drawings show person who is subject of the story (e.g., child, SLP) in every picture • **Fictional Stories** are acted out with toy miniatures as the story is told – language exactly matches actions • Story pictures are clear, uncluttered • Pictures closely match text; one picture per sentence • Language is concrete	• Stories are short; 3-4 sentences • Toys and pictures are used as memory cues during story retelling	• Bare-bones text: general story framework = character-action-feeling/coda	**Sentence Patterns:** • Subject-Verb • Subject-Verb-Object • Subject-Verb-Complement (e.g., He is happy. It is fun.) **Verb Tense:** Present tense; mostly present progressive	• Concrete nouns and verbs • Stories primarily contain words already in the child's repertoire • Basic emotion words (e.g., *happy, sad, mad, scared*)
Late Level I Stories						
	• **Fictional Stories** continue to be based on familiar routines and events the child has experienced but can be based on other events for which child has solid event knowledge	• 2-3 sentences may be associated with 1 story picture	• Stories increase in length to 4-7 sentences	Add ... • Beginning use of elaborated text	Add ... • Subject-Verb-Verb sentences • Prepositional phrases (usually no more than 1 per story) • Past tense may be introduced; mostly past progressive	Add ... • New verbs • Early mental state verbs • Negative: *not* • Modal: *can* • Time words: *now, next* • Adjectives and adverbs (sparingly)

Level II – Surprises

NURTURING NARRATIVES LEVELS		
	Tailored Stories personal narratives and fictional stories	**Story Lessons** narrative-based intervention sessions
	Level of Story Complexity	**Primary Focus**
Level I **Events**	**Low** Simple stories are based on familiar events and routines or recent personal experiences	• Engagement, joint attention, and reciprocal interaction • Interactive retelling of simple stories • Automaticity of basic sentence patterns • Internalization of a simple story framework
Level II **Surprises**	**Moderate** Stories begin to contain problems and solutions	• Early conversation skills • Independent retelling of stories in past tense • Expression of temporal and causal relationships in stories
Level III **Theory of** **Mind**	**High** Stories focus on characters' thoughts & perspectives	• Independence in simple conversations • Theory of mind skills • Expanded repertoire of complex sentences

Children are ready for Level II when they are able to …

- engage in joint story retelling

- produce simple sentences

- respond to simple questions

- understand basic emotion words

Children with language impairments tend to have difficulty expressing temporal and causal relationships in stories (Donaldson, Reid, & Murray, 2007; Reilly, Losh, Bellugi, & Wulfeck, 2004). These skills are targeted in Level II. Level II personal narratives and fictional stories are single episodes that begin to include problems, solutions, and character reactions. They are written with elaborated text as needed to facilitate the child's comprehension. The linguistic complexity and length of stories are systematically increased. Personal narratives are told with photographs or drawings; fictional stories continue to be told with toys and/or pictures. After practicing each story with visual supports, independent retelling of the story in past tense without visual cues is fostered.

Level of Support/Demand: Generally, the levels of support and demand are moderate as children begin to gain skills in retelling stories. Details of Level II story content are outlined in Table 4.2.

Nurturing Narratives Levels

Table 4.2

Tailored Story Components: Level II

Event Knowledge	Contextualization	Memory	Story Text	Syntax	Semantics
Early Level II Stories					
• Stories are based on routines and events for which the child has demonstrated event knowledge • Stories now contain a problem and a solution	• **Personal Narratives:** Story is told with photos (preferably) or drawings showing person who is the subject of the story (e.g., child, SLP) • **Fictional Stories** can be told while acted out with toy miniatures or as story pictures are viewed • Pictures are concrete; number of sentences to picture ratio varies from 1-5 sentences per picture	• Stories are retold from memory without visual or verbal cues after supported practice	• Elaborated text is used to (a) reduce need for inferencing, (b) provide background information, and (c) define new words	Add ... • Past tense	Add ... • Time words/phrases (e.g., *and then, at first, soon, last*) • More emotion words • Verbs of communication (e.g., *said, shouted, asked, whispered*) • Higher level mental state verbs (e.g., *think, know, guess, remember, forget, hope*) • Physical inferencing
Late Level II Stories					
			• Physical inferencing questions are sometimes inserted into story text	Add ... • Compound sentences containing *and, but,* and *so* • Complex sentences containing *because*	Add ... New vocabulary: • Continue to expand repertoire of verbs • Some "perceptually verbally explainable" words

Level III – Theory of Mind

	Tailored Stories personal narratives and fictional stories	Story Lessons narrative-based intervention sessions
NURTURING NARRATIVES LEVELS		
	Level of Story Complexity	**Primary Focus**
Level I **Events**	**Low** Simple stories are based on familiar events and routines or recent personal experiences	• Engagement, joint attention, and reciprocal interaction • Interactive retelling of simple stories • Automaticity of basic sentence patterns • Internalization of a simple story framework
Level II **Surprises**	**Moderate** Stories begin to contain problems and solutions	• Early conversation skills • Independent retelling of stories in past tense • Expression of temporal and causal relationships in stories
Level III **Theory of** **Mind**	**High** Stories focus on characters' thoughts & perspectives	• Independence in simple conversations • Theory of mind skills • Expanded repertoire of complex sentences

Children are ready for Level III when they are …

able to retell a simple problem-and-solution story *after hearing it one time*. On the first retelling, it is okay if the story contains a few minor errors, but it should include the following story features:

- identification of characters

- identification of setting (if relevant to the story)

- correct sequencing of story actions

- inclusion of story problem and solution

- reference to characters' internal states (may be limited to basic emotions)

Children are also expected to have begun to use the following syntactic forms:

- past tense verbs

- compound sentences with *and, but,* and *so*

- complex sentences with *because*

In Level III, children are exposed to longer and more complex single-episode stories. Emphasis is placed on understanding story characters' mental states, intentions, and motivations. As complex sentence patterns are needed to talk about people's mental states (Astington & Jenkins, 1999; Tager-Flusberg & Sullivan, 1994), comprehension and use of a variety of complex sentences is the second primary focus during this level.

Level of Support/Demand: The use of elaborated text is reduced as children demonstrate the ability to comprehend stories told with less supportive scaffolding. Children are also encouraged to create and share their personal narratives and retell fictional stories with greater independence. Details of Level III story content are outlined in Table 4.3.

Table 4.3

Tailored Story Components: Level III

Event Knowledge	Contextualization	Memory	Story Text	Syntax	Semantics
Early Level I Stories					
• Stories are based on any events for which the child has demonstrated event knowledge • Single-episode stories support comprehension of story characters' mental states, intentions, and motivations • "False-belief" stories	• Stories may still be told using figurines and toy miniatures but are usually not • Number of sentences to picture ratio varies; pictures may only loosely match text	• Single-episode stories are retold from memory without visual or verbal cues	• Elaborated text is used to (a) reduce need for inferencing, (b) provide background information, and (c) define new words • Social inferencing questions are sometimes built into the text	• Any complex sentence patterns child comprehends • Sentences containing sentential complements that express correct beliefs	• Time words: (e.g., *after, before*) • Some verbally explainable words • Higher level mental state verbs (e.g., *think, know, guess*) used in most stories • Physical and social inferences
Late Level I Stories					
• Stories may be based on events about which the child has incomplete knowledge or that are new to the child if expansion of event knowledge is the goal	• Stories become progressively decontextualized with inclusion of more abstract concepts that do not lend themselves to concrete visual representations		• Use of elaborated text is reduced, as the child shows readiness for a dialogic approach to clarifying text which is difficult to comprehend	**Add ...** • Sentences containing sentential complements that express "false beliefs"	**Add ...** • "False beliefs"

Chapter 5

Creating Tailored Stories

In this chapter you will find:

- The Tailored Stories Formula – a formula for creating stories that are manageable for children with CLP

- Four Steps to Creating Tailored Stories – guidelines for creating stories that "fit" the child

- Guidelines for training others to help children create personal narratives

- Samples of tailored personal narratives and fictional stories at three levels

A Formula for Tailored Stories

At the same time we want to create stories that children can successfully understand and retell, we also want the stories to function as a medium for teaching new skills, such as social communication, vocabulary, and syntax. In searching for the right balance of story elements to achieve this end, we have found that stories that are comprised mostly of components that are easily processed by the child plus one or two challenging elements generally work well.

Table 5.1 presents a sample story in which the Tailored Stories Formula was applied. In the story, several easily processed story components function to facilitate comprehension and production of the two more difficult story elements, and of the story as a whole.

Table 5.1

Tailored Stories Formula

Tailored Stories = mostly familiar, facilitating elements + 1 or 2 challenging elements

A Level II Example: "Spilled Juice"

This Level II story was told as it was acted out with realistic toy miniatures and retold using simple, uncluttered pictures:

"Here is a girl. She is drinking some juice. Uh oh, the girl is spilling the juice!

The girl is sad because she spilled her juice."

Elements in the Story That Facilitate Comprehension and Story Retelling:

- Story is based on a familiar event the child has directly experienced
- Story contains mostly familiar vocabulary and simple sentence patterns
- Story contains explicit language
- Story covers a short time span
- Story places low demand on child's memory capacity (i.e., contains only 4 sentences)
- Story comprehension and retelling are aided by concrete, contextualized, visual cues (e.g., story toys and pictures)

Elements in the Story That Are Challenging:

- Complex sentence expressing a causal relationship
- Understanding the relationship between story events and characters' feelings

The lower the functioning of the child, the more challenging the task of tailoring stories for him. The most common error is to make the challenge level too high. Try to err on the side of making the story too simple at first.

Four Steps to Creating Tailored Stories

Table 5.2 summarizes four steps involved in creating Tailored Stories and lists useful resources to aid in the process. Included in these resources are checklists and worksheets (described below) that are particularly helpful when first beginning to create Tailored Stories. After a little practice, however, readers will likely be able to plan a Tailored Story quickly using just the Tailored Story Worksheet (see page 77).

The **Nurturing Narratives Entry Level Checklist** (see Appendix C) involves answering a short set of questions to determine the general level of the child's story.

The **Event Knowledge Checklist** (see Appendix A) can be helpful in finding a theme or topic for the story which matches the child's background knowledge and interests.

The **Nurturing Narratives Goals** (see Appendix C) offer optional goals to target in the areas of Social Communication/Conversation, Receptive Language, Expressive Language, Telling Personal Narratives, Retelling Fictional Stories, Theory of Mind, and Story Play. Other goals from the child's therapy plan that are not on these lists may also be targeted in the story.

The three **Tailored Story Components charts** (found on pages 66, 69, 72 and in Appendix A) are organized by Nurturing Narratives Level (i.e., Level I, II, and III). They list optional story elements to target under each Tailored Story Component (Event Knowledge, Contextualization, Syntax, etc.).

The **Tailored Story Worksheet** (see Table 5.3 and Appendix A) offers a condensed one-page version of the three **Tailored Story Components charts.** When planning a Tailored Story, it is helpful to scan the worksheet and circle the elements one wishes to include in the story.

The steps listed in Table 5.2 may be used to tailor both personal narratives and fictional stories.

> **Several "fittings" may be needed before a favorable set of story features is determined for a child. The child's levels of understanding and engagement are key clues as to whether or not the right "story fit" has been found.**

Table 5.2

Four Steps to Creating Tailored Stories

	Steps	Useful Resources
Step 1: **Story Level**	Determine the general level (I, II or III) of the child's story	• Nurturing Narratives Entry Level Checklist (see Appendix C) • Chapter 4 – The Nurturing Narratives Levels
Step 2: **Story Theme**	Consider the child's interests and event knowledge when selecting the story topic	• Child observation • Parent report • Event Knowledge Checklist (see Appendix A) • Discussion of event knowledge beginning on page 30
Step 3: **Goals**	Choose the child's therapy goal(s) to be addressed in the story	• Child's language treatment plan • Goals listed in Appendix C
Step 4: **Tailored Story**	Using the Tailored Story Worksheet, identify key elements to include in the story. Create a story that contains mostly familiar language and concepts plus 1-2 challenging elements (see Tailored Stories Formula, Table 5.1)	• Tailored Stories Formula (see Table 5.1) • Tailored Story Components charts, (found on pages 66, 69, and 72, and in Appendix A) • Tailored Story Worksheet (see Table 5.3 and Appendix A) • Chapter 3 – The Tailored Stories Components

Creating Tailored Stories

Table 5.3

Tailored Story Worksheet

In each column, circle the items to be included/targeted in the story.

Event Knowledge	Contextualization	Memory	Story Text	Syntax	Semantics
Story is based on: • simple, *experienced* events • familiar *observed* events • *imaginary* events	**Story comprehension and retelling are supported by:** • life-size, realistic object replicas • dolls and miniature toy objects • photos • simple uncluttered pictures • 1 sentence per picture • 2 to 3 sentences per picture • pictures that less closely map text	**Story facilitates:** • autobiographical memory • event memory **Story length and complexity are controlled to:** • aid memory • challenge memory	**Text type:** • bare-bones text • elaborated text • unaltered text **Story length:** • 3 to 4 sentences • 5 to 10 sentences • length not controlled	**Sentence type:** • simple sentences: S-V, S-V-O, S-V-C, S-V-V • compound sentences with *and, but, so* • complex sentences with *because;* other coordinating conjunctions; sentential complements • prepositional or adverbial phrase **Verb tense:** • present progressive • present • past progressive • past • future	**Vocabulary:** • concrete nouns and verbs • basic emotions • early mental state terms • higher level mental state terms • verbs of communication • time words: *now, then, first, last, soon, after, before, when, while* **Inferencing:** • physical • social

Two Types of Tailored Stories

A Nurturing Narratives "Story Lesson" (see Chapter 7) consists of two segments, each focusing on a different type of story (personal narrative or fictional story). The session segments and stories are compared in Table 5.4.

Table 5.4

Comparison of Story Lesson Segments and Stories

Comparison of Story Lesson Segments and Stories		
Session Segment	**Sharing Personal Narratives**	**Understanding and Retelling Stories**
Session Description	Child and adult exchange stories about recent experiences in a conversational context	Story comprehension and retelling are addressed in the context of varied, interactive story repetitions
Story Type	Personal Narratives	Fictional Stories
Story Creation	The child and a "conversation facilitator" co-create the child's personal narrative The child's interventionist ("conversation partner") creates her own personal narrative	Stories are created by the interventionist

Same Levels of Story Complexity

The levels of cognitive and linguistic complexity of each type of narrative are kept the same throughout a given child's Story Lesson. In the early Level I sample stories below, one child's stories all have the same simple bare-bones structure (i.e., character–action–feeling/coda).

Early Level I		
Session Segment	**Story Type**	**Sample Stories**
Sharing Personal Narratives	Personal Narrative	This is me.* I am swimming. I am happy! *Story told while looking at photographs.*
Understanding and Retelling Stories	Fictional Narrative	"Here is a boy. He is eating ice cream. Yum!"

For another child, who is in late Level II, both types of narratives might include a problem and solution, a compound sentence, a complex sentence expressing causality, and past tense verbs.

Late Level II		
Session Segment	**Story Type**	**Sample Stories**
Sharing Personal Narratives	Personal Narrative	We went to the pool. Mom forgot my water wings. I was sad because I could not swim! Mom bought new water wings. Then I could swim. I was happy!
Understanding and Retelling Stories	Fictional Narrative	Drew was eating ice cream. Oh no, the ice cream fell on the ground! Drew said, "Mom, can I have more ice cream?" Mom gave Drew another ice cream cone. Drew was happy because he loves ice cream!

In the following sections, creation of Tailored Stories will be discussed, first with reference to personal narratives, then with reference to fictional stories.

Creating Tailored Personal Narratives

Many children with CLP attempt to tell personal narratives but are not very successful at conveying their thoughts in stories for a variety of reasons. These include difficulties with language formulation, story organization, and determining what background information their listeners need. Some children with more significant impairments do not attempt to talk about their experiences at all, or if they do, say only a word or two to tell their stories. All of these children could benefit from help in formulating and practicing their stories before telling them to others.

During the Sharing Personal Narratives segment of a session, the child and interventionist (or another conversation partner) tell each other stories about recent experiences they have had. This activity becomes more meaningful and pragmatically appropriate when the interventionist is able to recruit another person (like the child's parent, aide, or teacher) to act as a **conversation facilitator.** The primary role of the conversation facilitator is to help the child prepare a personal narrative to tell someone else.

Preparing the Child's Personal Narrative

Before the session, the conversation facilitator invites the child to remember and talk about a recent memorable experience. Visual cues such as photographs or simple drawings are offered to aid memory. Using the visual aids, the conversation facilitator helps the child create a personal narrative and practice telling it to his level of proficiency. Initially, this process is highly supported (e.g., the conversation facilitator may tell most of the story while the child listens and fills in a word or two). Over time, it is expected that the child will come to tell his story with greater independence.

Mentoring Conversation Facilitators

The person in the conversation facilitator role could be the SLP or another adult in the child's life whom the SLP has trained for this role. Parents, aides, and teachers are among people who are typically mentored to become conversation facilitators for the child.

In mentoring potential conversation facilitators, it is recommended that the SLP:

1. Discuss …
   * the importance of sharing personal narratives in our daily lives
   * the child's social, cognitive, and/or linguistic challenges that interfere with his ability to effectively share a story about a personal event with another
   * why the role of conversation facilitator is important
   * the ways in which successfully sharing personal narratives may benefit the child

2. Describe and show examples of stories that are appropriate for the child.

Additional resources to use when training others to help children create personal narratives to tell include "Guidelines for Co-Creating a Child's Personal Narrative" and the "Co-Creating Personal Narratives Worksheet" in Appendix A.

The Conversation Partner's Personal Narrative

The conversation partner's personal narratives are created at the same level as the child's Tailored Stories to ensure that the child understands the story. Pictures always accompany the conversation partner's Level I and Level II stories; they are optional in Level III. While drawings can be used, photographs are preferable, especially in Level I. Photographs, being more contextualized, are more likely to facilitate the child's association of the personal narrative with the storyteller as well as aid storage of the story in memory. Figure 5.1 shows an adult Level II personal narrative.

On Saturday, I wanted to ride in my kayak.

I was paddling.

Then I saw some big rocks. I was afraid! I was thinking I might bump into them!

Whew! I paddled around the rocks and did not bump them. I had fun kayaking on Saturday!

Figure 5.1. **A Level II adult personal narrative.**

Creating Tailored Personal Narratives at Three Levels

Level I – Events: Creating Tailored Personal Narratives with High Support

In Level I, the child is just being introduced to the process of creating personal narratives. Initially, the primary focus is on facilitating positive engagement and shared attention to the story pictures, as well as fostering the child's autobiographical memory. More emphasis is placed on language later in Level I.

Child's Level I Personal Narrative

Table 5.5 outlines the elements of the cognitive and linguistic complexity in children's Level I personal narratives.

Table 5.5
Child's Level I Personal Narrative

Cognitive Complexity	Linguistic Complexity
• Story is based on a recent simple experience, preferably one that elicited an emotional response from the child • Conversation facilitator uses photographs to aid comprehension and memory as the story is created and retold; the child appears in every picture • Conversation facilitator and child "co-tell" the story while referencing the story photographs; early on the child may attend but not yet verbalize • Later in Level I, the child may tell the story more independently using the pictures to aid story recall	• Story contains simple sentence patterns • Story generally contains vocabulary the child already knows • Inclusion of feeling words/codas is encouraged • Story is short, approximately 3-7 sentences long • Story can be told in present or past tense
Primary Goals for Level I Sharing Personal Narratives	
• Engagement, joint attention, and reciprocal interaction • Establishment of autobiographical memory • Interactive creation and retelling of personal narratives with high level of support	

Other goals may be found in Appendix C.

Verb Tense in Level I Personal Narratives

Personal narratives describe past events and, therefore, should be told in past tense language. However, sometimes it is preferable for the child's personal narrative to be told in the present tense. This is the case for children who do not understand the concept of the "past" or past tense language. It is also the case for children who understand the concept of telling a story about their past experiences but are not yet producing past tense language.

In late Level I when children are producing simple sentence patterns, the interventionist can begin to address past tense language production. After the child has shared his story one or more times using the story pictures as memory cues, the interventionist may remove the pictures and suggest they tell the story again together. The interventionist then prompts and produces recasts of the child's story to demonstrate correct production and facilitate imitation of past tense verbs.

| I have a bike. | I am riding. It's fun! |

Figure 5.2. Child's personal narrative – Early Level I sample: New bike.

| I was at the farmers market. | I was looking at the puppies. I wanted to pet them. | I was petting the puppies. It was fun! |

Figure 5.3. Child's personal narrative – Late Level I sample: Farmers market.

Conversation Partner's Level I Personal Narrative

- The conversation partner's stories are based on simple events that are familiar to the child.

- The cognitive and linguistic complexity of the conversation partner's story should match that of the child's story.

- As with the child's stories, the conversation partner's stories are always told with accompanying pictures. Drawings may be used; however, photographs that show the conversation partner in every picture are preferable, particularly in Level I (see Figure 5.4).

I got a present.	I was opening the present.
It was a game.	I love games! I was happy!

Figure 5.4. Conversation partner's personal narrative – Level I sample with photographs: Birthday present.

Level II – Surprises: Creating Tailored Personal Narratives with Moderate Support

As in Level I, the conversation facilitator invites the child to remember and talk about a recent memorable experience before the session. The conversation facilitator still offers visual cues to aid memory. In Level II, most children can relate to drawings and no longer require photographs for the pictures to be meaningful. Some children respond especially well when the conversation facilitator draws simple sketches as the remembered experience is talked about (Arwood & Kaulitz, 2007; Arwood, Kaulitz, & Brown, 2009).

We have found that when they are familiar with the context, almost all children can derive meaning from very cursory drawings that are only suggestive of the subject. However, if the child has a difficult time establishing autobiographical memory, as is the case with some children with ASD, it is recommended that photographs in which the child appears continue to be used.

Children are typically able to increase their participation in the creation and practice of their personal narratives in Level II. The conversation facilitator now usually helps the child practice telling the story to a level of independence and relative fluency before going to the session; during this practice, the child can continue to use the story pictures to aid memory of the story content and sequence.

Child's Level II Personal Narrative

Table 5.6 outlines the elements of cognitive and linguistic complexity in children's Level II personal narratives.

Table 5.6
Child's Level II Personal Narrative

Cognitive Complexity	Linguistic Complexity
• Story is based on a recent, memorable experience	**By the end of Level II:**
• Causality is highlighted; most stories contain a problem-solution or surprise-consequence	• Stories include compound sentences with *and, but*, and *so*, complex sentences with b*ecause*, and past tense verbs
• Visuals are used to aid comprehension and memory	• Stories can contain more emotion words and possibly verbs of communication and cognition
• The child tells the story with greater independence first with, then without, visuals in the past tense	• Stories are approximately 5-10 sentences long
Primary Goals for Level II Sharing Personal Narratives	
• Increased participation in creating personal narratives • Independent retelling of personal narrative after supported practice • Learning about others • Early conversation skills	

Other Level II goals may be found in Appendix C.

Patrick went to the park.	He took his robot.	Then Patrick lost his robot and he was sad.
Patrick and Mom were looking for the robot.	Then Patrick saw his robot.	Patrick was happy because he found his robot!

Figure 5.5. Child's personal narrative – Level II sample: Lost robot.

Conversation Partner's Level II Personal Narrative

- The conversation partner uses photographs or pre-prepared story drawings, or draws quick simple sketches while telling the story.

- The cognitive and linguistic complexity of the conversation partner's story matches that of the child's story.

I found a spider in my house. I like spiders but I do not want them in my house.	I caught the spider in a cup.	I put the spider outside. I was happy because the spider was outside.

Figure 5.6. Conversation partner's personal narrative – Level II sample:
A spider in the house.

Level III – Theory of Mind: Creating Tailored Personal Narratives with Low Support

In Level III, the child is now typically capable of creating more of his own personal narrative. At this stage, the conversation facilitator's help tends to focus on expanding the range of the child's sentence patterns and facilitating inclusion of more mental state vocabulary in the child's story.

Before the session, the conversation facilitator invites the child to remember and talk about a recent memorable experience that lends itself to talking about the child's and others' mental states. Thought bubbles are often used in story picture drawings to depict and facilitate comprehension of mental states.

In Level III, the children also often need help with organization, determining relevant information and/or recognizing the needs of the communication partner (for more information, explanation, etc.). Sequencing of pictures or written sentence strips and discussion of the conversation partner's probable background information on the topic are examples of activities that might be used to address these problems. Before the session, the conversation facilitator helps the child practice telling the story to his level of proficiency.

Child's Level III Personal Narratives

Table 5.7 outlines the elements of cognitive and linguistic complexity in children's Level III personal narratives.

Table 5.7

Child's Level III Personal Narrative

Cognitive Complexity	Linguistic Complexity
• Story is based on a recent personal experience • Story has a social focus (i.e., reference to own and others' mental states) • Conversation facilitator uses visuals (drawings with thought bubbles) and verbal explanation to aid comprehension of mental states and other abstract vocabulary • Child tells story first with, then without pictures	• Stories now include a variety of complex sentences • It is common for stories to have verbs of cognition (e.g., *think*, *know*, *guess*)
Primary Goals for Level III Sharing Personal Narratives	
• Reference to own and others' mental states/perspectives in stories • Independent retelling of personal narratives with less practice • Expanded use of complex sentences • Conversation skills	

Early Level III – Focus on Mental State Terms

Mom was looking for her purse. She was **worried** because she couldn't find it.	I **remembered** Mom put her purse in her bedroom.	I said, "Mom go look in your room."	Mom found her purse in her bedroom. She was **relieved**.

Figure 5.7. **Child's personal narrative – Early Level III sample: Mom's lost purse.**

Late Level III – Focus on False Belief

I was reading my book. It was really good.	Mom told me, "It's time to go to school.	I put my book on the table.	Then I went to school.
After school, I walked home. I was thinking about my book. I thought my book was on the table.	When I got home, I looked for my book. It was not on the table. I was confused.	Then Mom said, "I was cleaning up. I put your book on the bookshelf." I was glad I found my book.	

Figure 5.8. **Child's personal narrative – Late Level III sample: Missing book.**

Conversation Partner's Level III Personal Narrative

- The conversation partner uses prepared story pictures or draws them while telling the story. Mental states are often depicted in thought bubbles.

- The cognitive and linguistic complexity of the conversation partner's story matches that of the child's story.

- The conversation partner highlights mental states and uses elaborated language to define challenging words/concepts and reduce the need for inferencing.

Figure 5.9. Conversation partner's personal narrative – Level III sample: Lost keys.

Creating Tailored Fictional Stories at Three Levels

The second segment of a Nurturing Narratives session, Understanding and Retelling Stories, focuses on fictional stories. Fictional stories are prepared by the interventionist.

The cognitive and linguistic complexity of fictional stories matches that of the child's personal narratives at any given time. The Four Steps to Creating Tailored Stories (see Table 5.2) offers guidelines for creating both personal narratives and fictional stories; however, there are a few special considerations/recommendations to keep in mind when creating fictional Tailored Stories, as outlined in Table 5.8.

Table 5.8

Creating Fictional Tailored Stories: Special Considerations

Creating Fictional Tailored Stories: Special Considerations	
Event Knowledge	It is particularly important to consider a child's event knowledge when creating tailored fictional stories for lower functioning children.
Contextualization	Plan/prepare contextualized cues (e.g., toys, pictures, props) to support the child's engagement, comprehension and retelling of the story.
Verb Tense	For children who are in the process of learning about verb tense, it is recommended that a consistent system be used. For example, always tell stories in the present tense when acting them out with toys or as the story pictures are viewed, then tell the story in past tense when visual cues are removed.

Level I – Events: Creating Fictional Tailored Stories

Early Level I Bare-Bones Stories:

- are as simple as possible

- are based on a routine or event that is familiar to the child

- match the child's interests

- have a high level of contextualization

- are short (3-5 sentences)

- contain simple concrete language which is familiar to the child

Stories are created in this manner to facilitate the child's engagement and ability to process the story as a whole.

In late Level I, stories become slightly longer and less contextualized as new linguistic elements are gradually added. See Tailored Story Components: Level I chart in Appendix A for more specific details of Level I fictional stories.

Primary Goals for Level I – Understanding and Retelling Stories
• Expand repertoire of verbs • Establish automaticity of basic sentence patterns • Answer simple questions • Interactively retell simple stories • Reenact stories in play Other Level I goals may be found in Appendix C.

Early and Late Level I Tailored Fictional Stories

The stories depicted in Figures 5.10 and 5.11 are based on simple events familiar to most children. The later version demonstrates expansion of the first story with a slight increase in length and addition of a new sentence pattern (S-V-V). Elaborated text supports comprehension of early mental state terms/character's perspective. The later stories also represent a slight decrease in contextualized support with inclusion of more abstract vocabulary (*likes, wants*) and progression from one to two or three sentences relating to some pictures.

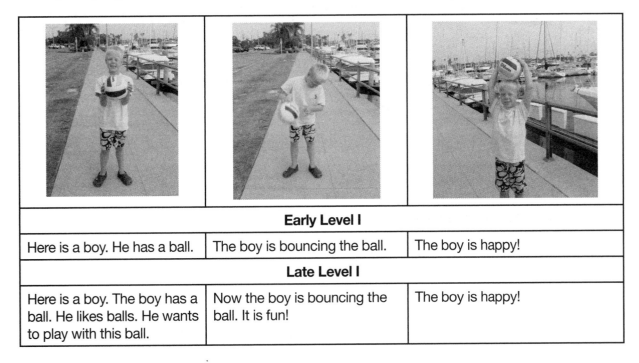

Early Level I		
Here is a boy. He has a ball.	The boy is bouncing the ball.	The boy is happy!
Late Level I		
Here is a boy. The boy has a ball. He likes balls. He wants to play with this ball.	Now the boy is bouncing the ball. It is fun!	The boy is happy!

Figure 5.10. Level I fictional story: Bouncing the ball.

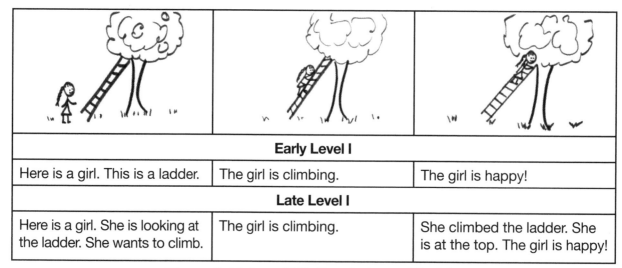

Early Level I		
Here is a girl. This is a ladder.	The girl is climbing.	The girl is happy!
Late Level I		
Here is a girl. She is looking at the ladder. She wants to climb.	The girl is climbing.	She climbed the ladder. She is at the top. The girl is happy!

Figure 5.11. Level I fictional story: Climbing.

Level II – Surprises: Creating Fictional Tailored Stories

Primary Goals for Level II – Understanding and Retelling Stories
• Express temporal and causal relationships in stories • Expand sentence patterns to include compound sentences (with *and, but,* and *so*) and complex sentences containing "because" • Independently retell stories with meaning Other Level II goals may be found in Appendix C.

Transition from Level I to Level II Stories: Addition of a Problem-Solution

One of the defining characteristics of a typical story is the "initiating event" – the part of the story that "kicks off the action" (Moreau & Fidrych, 2002, p. 30). In many stories, the initiating event is a problem that causes the main character to have an internal reaction and leads to one or more attempts to solve it.

In Level II, stories evolve from simple events to events that contain problems and solutions. When this component of complexity is first added, stories continue to be based on simple routines and events that are familiar to the child; often these are events the child has directly experienced.

The story in Figure 5.12 is based on an event that is familiar to most children, eating soup. In the Level I version of the story, the event is simply described. Then the same story event is expanded to introduce a familiar problem (spilling) and a solution to create a Level II story.

Creating Tailored Stories

Level I Version – Story Based on a Simple Event

Here is a girl.	She has soup and a spoon.	The girl is eating the soup. She likes it!

Level II Version — Addition of a Problem and Solution

Here is a girl.	She has soup and a spoon.	The girl is eating the soup. She likes it!
Uh oh, some soup is spilling.	The girl is sad because her shirt got dirty.	The girl put on a clean shirt, and now she is happy.

Figure 5.12. **Levels I and II fictional stories with simple drawings: Eating soup.**

The story in Figure 5.13 is based on a less familiar event, but one that some children find exciting, and hence engaging. For some pictures, optional text is offered in parentheses. In practice, the story text is tailored to the particular child's needs/goals.

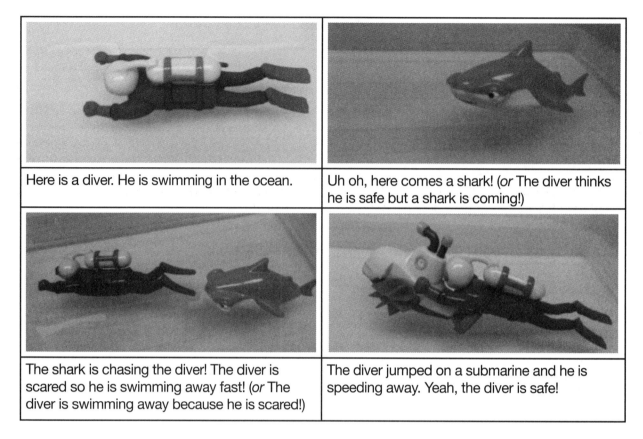

Here is a diver. He is swimming in the ocean.	Uh oh, here comes a shark! (*or* The diver thinks he is safe but a shark is coming!)
The shark is chasing the diver! The diver is scared so he is swimming away fast! (*or* The diver is swimming away because he is scared!)	The diver jumped on a submarine and he is speeding away. Yeah, the diver is safe!

Figure 5.13. **Level I fictional story with photographs of toys: The diver and the shark.**

From Lillian Vernon *Undersea Adventure Playset*.

Level III – Theory of Mind: Creating Fictional Tailored Stories

Primary Goals for Level III – Understanding and Retelling Stories
• Develop an increased ability to understand and talk about others' perspectives • Expand repertoire of complex sentences • Independently retell stories with less practice Other Level III goals may be found in Appendix C.

Creating Tailored Stories

Early Level III – Focus on Mental State Terms

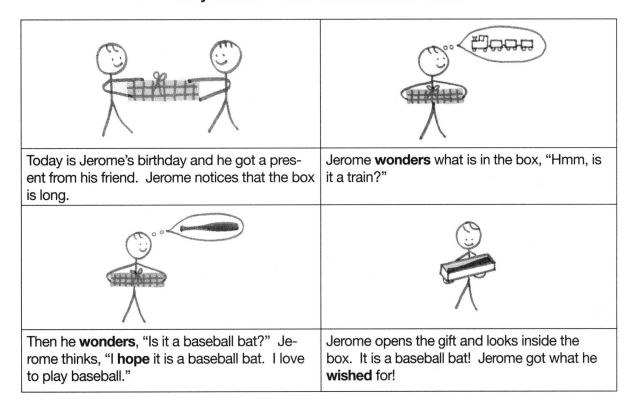

Today is Jerome's birthday and he got a present from his friend. Jerome notices that the box is long.	Jerome **wonders** what is in the box, "Hmm, is it a train?"
Then he **wonders**, "Is it a baseball bat?" Jerome thinks, "I **hope** it is a baseball bat. I love to play baseball."	Jerome opens the gift and looks inside the box. It is a baseball bat! Jerome got what he **wished** for!

Figure 5.14. **Early Level III fictional story: Jerome's birthday present.**

Late Level III – Focus on False Belief

Late Level III stories provide a vehicle for understanding and explaining differing perspectives and beliefs. The example in Figure 5.15 includes elaborated text and questions to facilitate comprehension of Mimi's false belief, which is based on not seeing something that is happening. Figure 5.16 provides another example of a false belief story.

Here is Mimi. She is hungry so she made a hamburger. She wants to eat it but first she wants to get some ketchup.

Mimi goes to the kitchen to get the ketchup. Here comes Joe and he sees the hamburger. Joe is thinking, "That hamburger looks good. I want to eat it!"

Joe starts eating Mimi's hamburger.

Does Mimi *see* Joe eating her hamburger?

Does she *know* Joe is eating it?

Now Mimi is ready to eat her hamburger. When she sees her hamburger is gone, she is surprised! She did not expect Joe to eat her hamburger! And now she is angry. Joe says, "I am sorry, Mimi. I will make another hamburger for you!"

Figure 5.15. Late Level III fictional story: Mimi's hamburger.

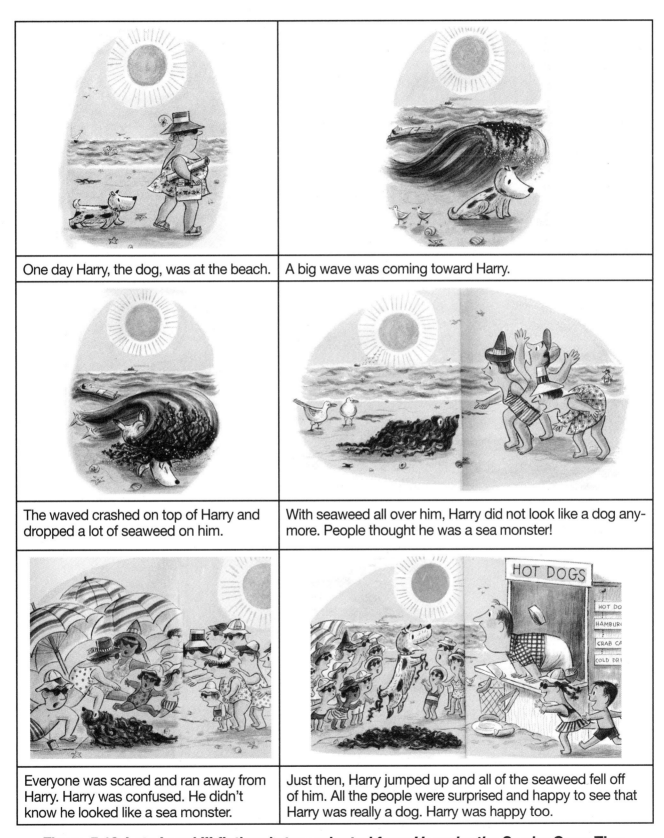

One day Harry, the dog, was at the beach.

A big wave was coming toward Harry.

The waved crashed on top of Harry and dropped a lot of seaweed on him.

With seaweed all over him, Harry did not look like a dog anymore. People thought he was a sea monster!

Everyone was scared and ran away from Harry. Harry was confused. He didn't know he looked like a sea monster.

Just then, Harry jumped up and all of the seaweed fell off of him. All the people were surprised and happy to see that Harry was really a dog. Harry was happy too.

Figure 5.16. **Late Level III fictional story adapted from *Harry by the Sea* by Gene Zion.**

Story Creation Resources in the Appendix on the Accompanying CD

Appendix A contains a variety of resources to aid in the creation of Tailored Stories. These include copies of the:

- Tailored Stories Components overview charts for each Level
- Tailored Stories Worksheet
- Event Knowledge Checklist
- Guidelines and Worksheet for Co-Creating a Child's Personal Narratives

Appendix A also includes recommendations for:

- Children's books that lend themselves to being adapted to create Tailored Stories
- Sequence picture box sets and workbooks
- Software for story creation
- Online story creation resources
- iPad, iTouch, and iPhone story creation applications

Appendix B includes sample Tailored Stories with Pictures in PowerPoint, ready for downloading and use in intervention sessions. These include:

- Nine stories from Chapter 5
- Sample stories for Early and Late Levels I, II, and III
- A Month of Stories – four stories that have sample texts for all Levels. The Month of Stories demonstrates how one can use one story per week with all children on one's caseload by adapting the story text to each child's level of functioning
- Three additional stories with sample texts for all Levels
- Four stories for story writing practice

Section III:
Nurturing Narratives Intervention

Section III includes information about:

- Fostering foundation skills for story-based intervention

- The two segments of a Story Lesson: Sharing Personal Narratives and Understanding and Retelling Stories

- Three levels of story-based intervention

Chapter 6

Fostering Foundation Skills for Stories

While stories are at the hub of the Nurturing Narratives approach, some children are not yet demonstrating one or more of the foundation skills for story-based intervention. Sometimes a child lacks knowledge about the events on which stories are based. At other times, the child is not demonstrating fundamental social interaction skills that are precursors to communication. In yet other cases, the child has not developed adequate language skills to understand the earliest Nurturing Narratives stories.

If a child has not acquired the skills listed in Table 6.1, it is recommended that these skills be addressed before or during the early stages of narrative-focused therapy.

Table 6.1
Foundation Skills for Story-Based Intervention

Foundation Skills for Story-Based Intervention
• Joint attention
• Turn taking – reciprocal interaction
• Event knowledge for familiar routines
• Intentional communication
• Imitation of simple actions and words
• A small vocabulary of concrete nouns and verbs

Low Verbal Joint Attention Routines

In Nurturing Narratives, development of the foundation skills for story-based intervention is addressed in the context of Low Verbal Joint Attention Routines (LVJARs). LVJARs are modeled after "joint action routines" or "JARs" (Snyder-McLean, Solomonson, McLean, & Sack, 1984), which focus on facilitating increased participation and communication during repeated, predictable routines. LVJARs also incorporate principles and practices of early intervention programs such as SCERTS – Social Communication, Emotional Regulation and Transactional Support (Prizant, Wetherby, Rubin, Laurent, & Rydell, 2006); DIR® – Developmental, Individual Difference, Relationship-Based/Floortime™ Model (Greenspan & Weider, 2006); Responsive Teaching (Mahoney & MacDonald, 2007); It Takes Two to Talk (Pepper & Weitzman, 2004); More Than Words (Sussman, 1999); and RDI – Relationship Development Intervention (Gutstein & Sheely, 2002).

- **LVJARs involve established routines in the child's life** (e.g., putting on socks and shoes, playing pat-a-cake) and/or new simple play routines that capture the child's attention and interest, like rolling a car down a ramp, stacking and knocking blocks, or blowing a hat off a doll's head. The intent is to engage the child in playful, reciprocal social interactions. A primary focus is on developing joint attention as that is what paves the way for all of the other foundational skills.

- **LVJARs are repeated over and over, like JARs.** Repetition facilitates establishment of event knowledge and autobiographical memory of the routine and provides opportunities to gradually scaffold greater degrees of the child's participation and acquisition of targeted skills.

- **LVJARs involve the use of real objects or life-size realistic replicas** as opposed to miniature replicas or substituted objects (e.g., a block to stand for a telephone), which are more abstract and may not be meaningful to a child at this stage.

- **When words are spoken during the routines, they are highly contextualized**; that is, they name objects and actions at moments when the child is attending to them.

Early Low Verbal Joint Attention Routines

Initially, no demands are placed on the child; rather, efforts are designed to entice the child's attention and participation. There is an emphasis on communicating acceptance, interest in the child, and desire to share a fun activity with him.

Early LVJARs are either nonverbal or minimally verbal. Many children at this level do not understand much of the language they hear around them. As a result, they may tune out spoken language or avoid it because it does not make sense and/or for reasons related to sensory sensitivities. However, although spoken language is kept to a minimum, there is a heightened use of nonverbal communication. Positive affect, interest, approval, invitations to join the play, reactions to what is happening, and so on, are all communicated through exaggerated facial expressions, gestures, and simple vocalizations like "ooh!," "hmm?" and "wee!" Decreasing verbal communication that is not meaningful to the child and increasing visual communication can encourage the child to look at and interact with the play partner.

As LVJARs are repeated several times, the child has multiple opportunities to participate in the routine in different ways (like sharing positive affect, initiating shared emotion, performing actions in the routine, directing the other's actions, and/or saying a relevant word).

Later Low Verbal Joint Attention Routines

As children demonstrate increased participation, performance of the routine, and comprehension, the language associated with the routines is gradually increased to include phrases and simple sentences of approximately three to four words in length. Opportunities are offered for the children to imitate words and phrases and produce one to three word utterances to label, request, comment, command, and so on.

The following is a description of a LVJAR being conducted by Jenny, an SLP, with Simon, a 5-year-old, minimally verbal boy who has a diagnosis of autism and cognitive delay.

Sample Low Verbal Joint Attention Routine: "Blowing Hats"

Materials: doll, doll's hat (lightweight)

Routine: place hat on doll, blow the hat, hat blows/falls off

Text Progression:

- Nonverbal communication only
- Single words: e.g., *girl/boy, hat, blow, on, off*
- 2-word phrases: e.g., *blow hat, put on, fall off*
- 3-word phrases: e.g., *blow hat off, put on hat, hat fell off*
- Simple sentences: e.g., Here is a girl/boy. She/He has a hat. I am blowing. The hat fell off!

Introducing the Routine Nonverbally

Jenny attempts to draw Simon's attention to herself, the objects she is interacting with, and the actions she is performing by acting excited as she presents the doll and hat and puts the hat on the doll, while constantly alternating her gaze between the child and toys as if to <u>nonverbally</u> say, "Oh look! Look at these toys! I have an idea! It's going to be exciting/fun/cool/funny! Okay now watch! Are you ready? Are you watching? I'm almost ready to show you!"

Jenny draws out the introduction to the central action of the routine to build dramatic expectation and lengthen Simon's participation in joint attention. Jenny takes three theatrical in-breaths, pauses again while she still continually shifts her gaze between Simon and the toys, and then dramatically blows the hat off the doll. She acts delighted, laughs joyfully, and shows keen interest in observing Simon's reaction. Her nonverbal communication now says, "That was so funny! Don't you think so too? Wasn't that great? Did you like it? Doesn't it look like fun?!"

Facilitating Establishment of Event Knowledge

Jenny shifts to offering Simon a turn, as she nonverbally says with looks and gestures, "Hey, I have an idea! Why don't you try? Do you want a turn? Do you want to blow the hat? Yes, yes, do that! It's your turn!" Jenny places the hat on the doll and turns the doll toward Simon, nodding and smiling. Jenny models blowing if needed and blows the hat off the doll for Simon if he does not attempt to do so himself. Then she indicates she wants another turn, again with drama and excitement and constant alternating of gaze between the child and toys.

As the routine continues to be repeated, Jenny creates opportunities for Simon to demonstrate that he is beginning to internalize a script of the event. For example, she pauses before blowing the hat to see if Simon looks at the hat in anticipation of it flying off the doll's head. She also provides opportunities for Simon to perform more and more of the routine as he is able.

> *Slowly Attaching Language to the Routine*
>
> When Simon is engaged and has started to participate in the routine, Jenny begins to introduce some key words into the routine, for example, "Blow!" just before or during blowing, and "hat" as she hands Simon the hat. She asks "hat?" when the hat has blown off the table; Jenny feigns confusion and wonder about the disappearance of the hat. Her single questioning word and actions seem to ask Simon, "What happened to the hat?! Where did it go?!" Jenny also says *on* and *off* as the hat goes on and comes off the doll's head. These words will later be expanded into the verbs *put on* and *fall off*. She limits targeted words to concrete nouns and verbs of motion.
>
> Jenny monitors Simon's comprehension of the spoken words and only introduces more into the routine as earlier words appear to be meaningful to him. As Simon demonstrates comprehension of the single words that Jenny says, she gradually increases the length of her utterances to three-word phrases and simple sentences to express a variety of communicative intents. Jenny regularly pauses to allow opportunities for Simon to imitate, finish a phrase she has started, or initiate a verbalization on his own. For example, when Jenny waits for a moment once poised to blow the hat, Simon might say, "Blow!"

Goals for Low Verbal Joint Attention Routines

A set of intervention goals that might be targeted during intervention to establish foundation skills for stories appears in Appendix C. The major goal areas are summarized below.

Social Goals

Engagement, engagement, engagement! Moments of shared attention, shared expectation, and shared emotion are highly sought after. When possible, such moments are held and extended. A key aim is to help the child build positive memories associated with interacting with us.

Goals also focus on facilitating the child's skills for responding and initiating within social interactions. These include skills for attending to others and monitoring their actions and reactions, initiating and responding to requests for joint attention, and participating in extended reciprocal interactions.

Cognitive Goals

Through positive engagement in repeated LVJARs, we want to help the child establish event memories (i.e., mental scripts for the routines). At the same time, we are facilitating the child's ability to perform the actions of the routine, and to do so in correct sequence.

Communication/Language Goals

These goals focus on facilitating attention to, and comprehension of, nonverbal communication along with attachment of meaningful language to familiar routines. There is an emphasis on building the child's comprehension and use of basic nouns and verbs, and on eliciting verbal imitation.

Monitoring Progress During Low Verbal Joint Attention Routines

During the LVJAR, the interventionist looks for indications that the child is developing the foundational skills he will need in order to participate meaningfully in story-based intervention. These include signs that the child is developing event knowledge for the routine. For example, the interventionist watches to see if the child is starting to anticipate what will happen next in the routine. She also pauses at key moments to see what part(s) of the routine the child can both initiate and perform. For example, the child might start an action in the routine but need help to complete it, or he might perform the whole sequence of actions in the routine independently.

The interventionist also looks for signs of emerging social skills – Does the child attend to the adult with greater frequency or longer durations? Does the child look to the adult for a response after performing an action in the routine? Does the child respond to the adult's attempts to direct the child's focus of attention? Does the child direct the adult's attention? The interventionist regularly pauses to observe whether the child will imitate, finish a phrase she has started, or initiate a verbalization on his own.

The Goal/Progress Monitoring forms in Appendix C are a useful resource for tracking a child's progress.

Activities for Low Verbal Joint Attention Routines

Any activity that facilitates the child's engaged interaction with the adult may be shaped into an LVJAR with a predictable sequence for the child. Table 6.2 lists activities related to familiar daily routines and play routines that might lend themselves to creating an LVJAR.

Table 6.2

Activities for Low Verbal Joint Attention Routines

Activities for Low Verbal Joint Attention Routines	
• Tickling games	• Pouring a drink
• Chasing games	• Putting peanut butter on a cracker
• Hiding under bean bag chairs	• Mixing lemonade
• Peek-a-boo	• Washing a dirty toy
• Rough-housing games	• Fixing a broken toy
• Songs with actions ("Ring-Around-the-Rosie," "Itsy Bitsy Spider")	• Taking off, hiding, finding, and putting on shoes
• Swinging in arms or in swing	• Engaging in ball activities
• Riding in wagon face to face	• Stacking and knocking down blocks
• Dancing to music	• Playing with cars and ramp
• Holding hands, looking at each other, and jumping off a step at the same time	• Hitting balloons with paddles
	• Blowing up and releasing a balloon
• Placing object on head; tilting head to make object fall	• Blowing cotton balls across the table through straws
• Playing with wind-up/spinning/squirting/flying toys	• Blowing hat off doll
• Requesting more food/drink	• Placing doll in wagon, pushing, then tipping the wagon
• Spilling water and cleaning up	

Transition to Stories

Early Level I stories often involve using people dolls to act out the routines the child partici-pated in during LVJARs. This progression represents a small step along the contextualized to decontextualized continuum. The language used to talk about actions the child is observ-ing and performing during play routines is more contextualized, and hence less abstract, than language that describes actions one performed in the past or actions of dolls (symbolic people).

Following is an example of a routine narrated with language, followed by a simple personal narrative and a simple fictional story based on that routine.

Late LVJAR

Here is a car. Look, a ramp! Push! Push the car. Zoom!

Alternate text:

I have a car. Here is a ramp. I am pushing. Ooh! The car is going!

Early Level I Personal Narrative (told while viewing photographs of the activity)

I have a car. This is a ramp. I am pushing the car. The car is going!

Early Level I Fictional Story (told while acting the story out with toy miniatures)

Here is a boy. He has a car. He has a ramp. The boy is pushing the car.
The car is going!

Chapter 7

Story Lessons

"Go for the gleam in the eye."

Greenspan & Lewis (2005, p. 149)

Nurturing Narratives language intervention sessions are called **Story Lessons**. During Story Lessons, children's social, cognitive, and linguistic skills are nurtured in the context of enticing story-centered interactions. Story Lessons are typically conducted in two segments, **Sharing Personal Narratives** and **Understanding and Retelling Stories**. The content and focus of the two segments are compared in Table 7.1.

Table 7.1

Comparison of Sharing Personal Narratives and Understanding and Retelling Stories

STORY LESSONS		
Session Segment	**1. Sharing Personal Narratives**	**2. Understanding and Retelling Stories**
Story Type	Personal Narratives	Fictional Stories
Description	Child and adult exchange stories about their recent experiences in a conversational context	Story comprehension and retelling are addressed in the context of varied, interactive story repetitions
Key Focus	Expansion of pragmatic skills	Expansion of receptive and expressive language
Similarities	<ul><li>Top priority: Engagement</li><li>Level of story complexity</li><li>Focus on mastery of new skills</li></ul>	

Segment I: Sharing Personal Narratives

When friends meet, they often exchange stories about recent events in their lives, and those stories tend to spark conversation. During the Sharing Personal Narratives segment of the Story Lesson, acquisition of skills for participating in this common and important, yet complex, social-communicative activity is addressed.

Exchanging stories about personal experiences and discussing them can be particularly challenging for many children with CLP due to the compounded complexity of narratives and conversation. Some research indicates that children with ASD additionally have difficulty establishing autobiographical memories – memories about their own experiences – that form the content for personal narratives (Millward, Powell, Messer, & Jordan, 2000).

When children with CLP are first introduced to Sharing Personal Narratives, many of them are not very verbal. In addition, they may not seek social interaction because of the severity of their communication or sensory processing problems and/or difficulties with social relatedness. Early on, the process of Sharing Personal Narratives is significantly simplified and specially scaffolded to make the child's meaningful participation possible. Initially, emphasis is placed on fostering social engagement and positive emotions associated with this activity. Then aspects of complexity are added, and supports are withdrawn as the child demonstrates growth of new skills and readiness for higher levels of independence in sharing and talking about personal stories (see Table 7.2).

Table 7.2
Sharing Personal Narratives

Early Focus	Later Focus
• Strengthening autobiographical memories • Joint attention • Sharing emotions • Turn taking • Language comprehension	• Expressive language • Story organization • Thinking and learning about the communication partner • Topic maintenance • Reciprocal conversation

"Tell a Story to Get a Story"

During the Sharing Personal Narratives segment of the session, we often use a strategy called "Tell a Story to Get a Story," described by McCabe and Rollins (1994). This involves an adult (SLP, teacher, parent, other) telling the child a story about an experience she has had, and then inviting the child to tell his personal narrative. While McCabe and Rollins used this strategy to elicit spontaneous narratives from preschoolers for research purposes, in Nurturing Narratives it is used to foster a natural-feeling communicative exchange between the child and adult.

Another way in which Sharing Personal Narratives differs from the McCabe and Rollins (1994) procedure is that the child's personal narratives are not completely spontaneous, at least during the early levels. That is, the child's stories are usually prepared and practiced before the Story Lesson, as described in Chapter 5 and briefly reviewed in this chapter.

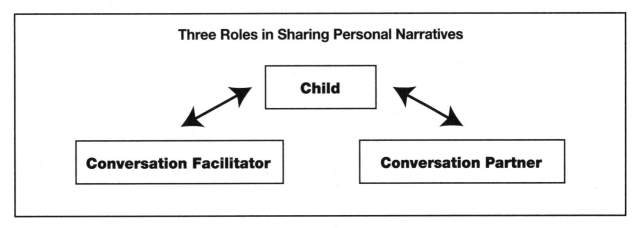

Figure 7.1. Three roles in Sharing Personal Narratives.

The Sharing Personal Narratives process proceeds best when three people are involved – the child, a conversation facilitator, and a conversation partner. Often a child's parent, teacher, or instructional aide acts as the conversation facilitator, and the SLP acts as the conversation partner, but the roles may be switched.

As discussed in Chapter 5, the conversation facilitator and conversation partner each play a role in creating tailored personal narratives before the Story Lesson. They also have roles during the Sharing Personal Narratives segment of the Story Lesson:

- The **conversation facilitator** helps the child prepare a personal narrative before the session to tell to the conversation partner (during the session) and also scaffolds the child's participation in conversation about the personal narratives that the child and conversation partner exchange during the Story Lesson.

- The **conversation partner** is the person to whom the child tells his personal narrative, the person who tells the child a personal narrative of his or her own, and the person who converses with the child about the stories they have exchanged. It is preferable for the child to gain experience communicating with a variety of conversation partners.

Three Parts in Sharing Personal Narratives

Table 7.3 lists the three parts of Sharing Personal Narratives.

Table 7.3
Three Parts of Sharing Personal Narratives

Part 1	Story Preparation
Part 2	Conversation
Part 3	Story Practice

Part 1: Story Preparation

The process of preparing tailored personal narratives and guidelines for training others to be conversation facilitators are reviewed in Chapter 5, Creating Tailored Stories. To recap here briefly, before the session, the conversation facilitator uses visual cues like photographs and drawings to help the child recall a recent personal experience and create a story about it to tell later to the conversation partner. The conversation facilitator then helps the child practice telling the story to the level of proficiency the child can attain.

Prior to the session, the conversation partner also prepares a personal narrative to tell to the child. This story matches the level of complexity of the child's story.

Part 2: Conversation

> "Participation in verbal exchanges requires basic conversational skills. Primary among these are (a) the ability to initiate an interaction (assertiveness) and (b) the ability to appropriately respond to and thereby maintain an interaction (responsiveness) … Greenwood, Walker, Todd, and Hops [1981] and his colleagues found that by age 3 children are successful in obtaining and providing reciprocity in peer interaction more than 90% of the time."
>
> Hadley & Rice (1991, p. 1308)

As mentioned, when friends get together, they tend to start out by "catching up" – sharing news about what has been happening in their lives. A primary intent in beginning Story Lessons with Sharing Personal Narratives is to mirror this type of conversation.

A Conversation Framework

The process of exchanging personal narratives is embedded in the conversation framework presented in Table 7.4 for a couple of reasons. First, doing so places the telling of personal narratives in a meaningful, pragmatically appropriate context. Second, repeated exposure to the same framework helps some children internalize it, at least in part. **An internalized conversation framework may have a general effect of helping to reduce the processing load for participation in conversations.**

The conversation framework in Table 7.4 includes not only the conversation partner's and child's stories, but also transitions between the two. For many children with CLP, it is the transitions – the means of tying the conversation together – that are particularly challenging. The aim is to facilitate not only the child's ability to respond and initiate but also to gain a sense of, and some skills for, "keeping the conversation going."

Table 7.4

Conversation Framework

Conversation Framework
• Initiate and respond to greetings.
• Transition to first story with a leading comment/question (e.g., "I went on a trip.") and a related response (e.g., "Oh, where did you go?).
• Tell first story.
• Engage in reciprocal exchanges about first story.
• Transition to second story.
• Tell second story.
• Engage in reciprocal exchanges about second story.

Nurturing Narratives

Early on, the child's participation in the conversation is highly supported. If the conversation facilitator can be present in the session, she may join the conversation as a third participant and model and cue appropriate utterances. Later, some whispered cues from the sidelines might suffice. The SLP coaches the conversation facilitator in how to scaffold the exchange. When a conversation facilitator can be present to act in this role, the child is able to experience a more pragmatically typical conversation, one in which the conversation partner is (seemingly) not privy in advance to the information the child is communicating. However, when a conversation facilitator cannot be present, the interventionist directly scaffolds the conversation.

As children gain familiarity with the framework, they are presented with opportunities to spontaneously respond and initiate elements in the conversation. For example, initially the conversation partner is likely the one to greet the child first; however, in time she may refrain from saying anything when the child arrives and, instead, smile and look expectantly to see if the child might be the first to say "hello."

Scaffolding Transitions in Conversation

Randy is a 10-year-old boy with ASD who, after participating in many supported conversations, now initiates greetings when he arrives at his therapy sessions. Then after the exchange of greetings, he will announce his story (e.g., "I went bowling."). His SLP may say something like "You went bowling?!" and Randy then spontaneously tells his story.

In the past when he finished his story, Randy made no move to keep the conversation going. At this time he still does not spontaneously think to ask about his conversation partner – a good conversational strategy – but he is learning to do so. Now when he comes to the end of his personal narrative, his SLP looks at him with an interested and expectant expression on her face, and after a few seconds Randy will ask, "What have you been doing?" This transition in the conversation is not yet smooth or automatic, but when Randy remembers what to say, he seems proud of himself and more invested in listening to his conversation partner's story.

In addition to exchanging and talking about new personal narratives, memory and reference to previous personal narratives may be facilitated during Sharing Personal Narratives. The SLP models remembering and asking questions related to what she knows about the child (e.g., "How is your hamster? Did she get out of her cage again!?"). The child's memory and questions about the conversation partner's stories are scaffolded as needed. The goal for some children will be that one day they will spontaneously ask a question like, "Did you ride in your kayak (this week)?"

As discussed, pragmatic skills are targeted during the conversation phase of Sharing Personal Narratives. The interventionist may respond to language errors with "recasts," but she will not interrupt the flow of the exchange to address correction of syntax. If needed, language errors are addressed during Part 3 – Story Practice.

Part 3: Story Practice

Even though the child has practiced the personal narrative before the Story Lesson, he may not yet tell it at the level of proficiency the SLP would like. In such cases, the interventionist may facilitate further practice of the child's story after the conversation phase (Part 2). During story practice, skills like syntax and story organization can be scaffolded. For example, after the "conversation," the interventionist may say, "I love your story! I want to hear it again." Or she might ask if the child can retell the story without using the pictures.

Story retelling expectations in each Level, along with strategies for facilitating repeated practice of stories, are discussed later in this chapter in the section titled Segment II: Understanding and Retelling Stories.

Maintaining the child's engagement and repeated practice of a story until it is mastered are two key goals in Nurturing Narratives, but achieving both can pose a challenge with some children.

It is important, first of all, to use personal narratives that are well matched to the child in terms of both language ability and interest. Then the challenge is to present the task in ways that motivate the child. Below are some strategies that were found to be effective with one child; different combinations tend to work with different children, so some experimentation with various strategies is often needed. Other strategies for facilitating repeated story practice are found on pages 133-136.

Facilitating Story Practice with a Boy Who Did Not Like to Practice Stories!

Matthew was a child who was particularly resistant to telling his story a second, much less a third or fourth, time. He was a bright, energetic, and extremely personable 7-year-old who was enthralled with insects. His family spoke their native language at home; another non-English language was the primary language at his school, where Matthew was in the first grade. He had a diagnosis of attention deficit-hyperactivity disorder (ADHD), and testing revealed significant delays in his first language, the language used in his school, and English.

Matthew seemed acutely aware of his difficulties with language production and appeared to try to "cover them up." He tended to engage in extended monologues as if he were telling a long story or giving a lengthy opinion on some matter. His delivery was full of theatrical gesture and inflection but, sadly, most of the time, nobody could understand what he said. When a listener expressed lack of understanding, Matthew acted exasperated and insulted. It appeared that his difficulty with language was negatively affecting his self-concept, and referral to a child psychologist was recommended. Meanwhile it was a challenge to get Matthew to retell a story and be receptive to feedback while doing so.

One day Matthew's older brother caught a grasshopper but lost it again. Matthew was thrilled when he caught the grasshopper himself and it stayed on his hand for a long time. Before his Story Lesson that day, Matthew's mother helped him prepare a personal narrative about the experience. When Matthew arrived at the session, he was excited to tell his story, but it was very hard to understand. The story pictures his mother had drawn were wonderful but too detailed to serve as an aid to remembering the critical parts of the story, and the language she had chosen for the story was too complex for Matthew. (Creating stories that are too difficult for the child is typical, particularly in the early stages of Sharing Personal Narratives. When that happens, the interventionist should mentor the conversation facilitator in how to revise the story to make it more manageable for the child.)

As usual, Matthew was resistant to clarifying his story when first asked. His SLP said she really liked the story and wanted to draw some pictures of it. She asked him to help her by telling her what to draw. Matthew struggled to find and sequence the words in sentences. His SLP found that it helped him to have visuals that represented the different parts of the sentences when one picture to represent each whole sentence did not work. She also provided only the visual details that served as direct cues for the wording needed. The SLP used different colors for each sentence of the story when Matthew's performance indicated he was not clear on where each sentence began and ended.

Although these visual cues seemed as if they could provide effective scaffolding for Matthew to tell his story, he was still resistant to retelling it until his SLP hit on the idea of having him manipulate a "grasshopper" (which she quickly fashioned from a green index card) while he told the story. Matthew took great pleasure in making the grasshopper jump away from his brother. Each time Matthew gleefully threw the grasshopper into the air, his SLP joined him by matching his joyful affect, which seemed to help him maintain his enthusiasm.

Matthew particularly struggled with correct use of prepositions and conjunctions in his story. It helped him to pair the act of placing the grasshopper on his hand with saying the phrase "on my hand." Since the preposition *with* and the conjunction *but* could not be pictured or acted out, the SLP had written them in large letters. Matthew was not yet reading, but putting these written words on separate cards helped to distinguish them as distinct components of the sentences they were in.

Visual Cues for Matthew's Grasshopper Story:
Stickwriting, Key Words, and Color-Coded Sentences

I was at the playground   with   my brother Jason.   Jason saw a grasshopper.

Jason was catching the grasshopper   but   the grasshopper jumped away.

I caught the grasshopper.   He sat on my hand for a long time.

I was happy but Jason was sad.

These strategies helped Matthew stay engaged through several repetitions of the story, and his performance improved in different ways with each repetition. However, he tired of the activity before reaching a point where he could tell the story to someone else and experience the pleasure of being understood.

Knowing how much Matthew seemed to enjoy "being on stage," his SLP told him again that she loved the story and asked if she could please videotape him telling it. He liked this idea, but his performance was still not to the level his SLP wished, and she wanted him to practice it one more time. So she lied to him! She told him she had goofed and not turned on the video camera correctly and asked him if he would please, please tell the story just one more time.

Her ploy worked, and he got another practice round. When his mother returned to pick him up, she was told the story, and Matthew even wanted to take the story home and tell it to his father. Finding the right scaffolding motivated Matthew to practice his story to "mastery," have fun, and gain a sense of accomplishment in the process.

Sharing Personal Narratives Through the Levels

Level I: Events – Sharing Personal Narratives with High Support and Low Demand

Primary Goals for Level I Sharing Personal Narratives
• Engagement, joint attention, and reciprocal interaction
• Establishment of autobiographical memory
• Interactive creation and retelling of personal narratives with high level of support

Part 1: Story Preparation

During Level I, the conversation facilitator helps the child prepare a personal narrative based on a simple recent experience before the Story Lesson. (Guidelines for creating Personal Narratives may be found in Chapter 5.)

Part 2: Conversation

Although children are not yet ready for true conversation in Level I, it is desirable to begin to foster aspects of conversation by modeling and creating opportunities for pragmatically appropriate initiating and responding. In the beginning, children generally participate in sharing personal narratives in simple ways. For example, they jointly attend to the story pictures and share an emotion about the story (as in mirroring the conversation partner's facial expression when that person says utterances like "It was icky!" or "I was surprised!"). When it is time for the child's story, he usually participates by completing the conversation facilitator's sentences with one to two words.

In Level I conversations, care is taken not to overwhelm the child with too much language. Table 7.5 shows the conversation framework applied to Level I.

Table 7.5
Creating Conversation in Level I

Creating Conversation in Level I	
• **Exchange greetings**	Upon seeing the child at the start of the session, the conversation partner smiles and pauses a moment to let the child be the first to greet; if the child does not, the conversation partner initiates the exchange of greetings.
• **Transition to 1st story**	The conversation partner says a leading comment (e.g., "I did something fun."), pauses briefly for a possible response, and then tells his or her own story.
• **Tell 1st story**	The child attends to the conversation partner's story – no other response is expected.
• **Transition to 2nd story**	At the end of the story, the conversation partner looks expectantly and shifts gaze between the child and the child's story pictures to allow the child a chance to initiate his own story. If the child does not initiate, the conversation partner invites the child's story with an animated leading comment like, "You did something ..."
• **Tell 2nd story**	While the child's story is told (often with the help of the conversation facilitator), the conversation partner shows attention and interest with body language, facial expressions, "mm-hm's," "oh's," and "wow's." The conversation partner does not interrupt the child's story by saying anything other than one-word indications of interest since the need to process the conversation partner's utterance could derail the child's story.
• **Engage in reciprocal exchanges about 2nd story**	After the child has completed the story, the conversation partner may make a simple comment; no questions are asked during Level I Sharing Personal Narratives.

Part 3: Story Practice

At the outset, emphasis is placed on experiencing a simple, pleasurable social-communicative exchange with no to low demand for language performance on the child's part. Later in Level I, some children are capable of producing more of their own personal narratives independently with the aid of their story pictures. Table 7.6 gives an overview of Level I personal narratives.

Difficulty Understanding Others' Personal Narratives

Some children find stories about their own experiences meaningful, but due to lower cognitive or perspective-taking ability, they do not understand others' personal narratives. Roy, for example, is a 15-year-old boy with ASD who likes others to listen to his simple stories about his experiences. However, when others tell him stories about their experiences, his responses imply that he understands the story to be about himself, not them. With children like Roy, listening to others' stories is not included as part of their narrative intervention program since it is not a meaningful activity for them.

Story Lessons

Table 7.6
Overview of Level I Personal Narratives

Level I	Child's and Conversation Partner's Personal Narratives	
Cognitive Complexity	• Story based on a simple, recent, pleasurable event • Story describes a short time span • Stories vary in length but are usually no more than 4 sentences • Visuals (preferably photos) are used during story telling; pictures closely match story and are shown one at a time • Early on, the conversation facilitator takes lead in "co-telling" story with child • Conversation facilitator may pause for child to finish sentences with 1-2 words, but completes sentence if child does not spontaneously participate • Later in Level I, child may produce more of story independently using pictures to aid memory	
Linguistic Complexity	• Story contains simple sentences and vocabulary which the child comprehends • Story can be told in present or past tense • Story includes a simple emotion or coda (e.g., "It was fun!")	
Sample Stories	**Child's**	**Adult's**
	1. This is me. I am eating pizza. It is good! – or – I ate pizza. It was good! 2. I went to the park. I was sliding. I was happy!	1. I went swimming. I was happy! 2. I went to a movie. I saw Nemo. It was good!
Conversation		
• Upon seeing the child, the conversation partner smiles and pauses a moment to let the child greet first; if the child doesn't, the conversation facilitator initiates exchange of greetings. • Conversation partner says a leading comment (e.g., "I did something fun!"), pauses briefly for a possible response, then tells own story. • Child attends to the conversation partner's story – no other response is expected. • Conversation partner looks expectantly at child to allow chance for child to initiate own story; if child does not initiate, conversation partner "invites" child's story with an animated leading comment like "You did something …" • While child's story is told, conversation partner shows attention and interest with body language and facial expressions. • Conversation partner may make a simple comment at the end but does not interrupt child's story; no questions are asked.		

Level II Surprises – Sharing Personal Narratives with Moderate Support and Demand

Primary Goals for Level II – Sharing Personal Narratives
• Increased participation in creating personal narratives
• Independent retelling of personal narrative after supported practice
• Learning about others
• Early conversation skills

Part 1: Story Preparation

During Level II, the conversation facilitator helps the child prepare a personal narrative based on a recent experience that preferably involved a simple problem and a solution. Typically, the child is able to offer more during creation of the story than in Level I. (Guidelines for creating personal narratives may be found in Chapter 5.)

Part 2: Conversation

When the child arrives at the session, the conversation partner usually tells the first personal narrative and then invites a story from the child. After several experiences with sessions beginning in the same way, many children begin to anticipate the request for their personal narratives. And, having already practiced with a conversation facilitator, many are motivated to tell their stories. Often they reference their story pictures to help them tell their stories, but in time, some no longer need the visual cues.

In Level II, children can usually tell their personal narratives with a higher level of independence (i.e., with less help from the conversation facilitator) than in Level I. They also begin to participate more in "conversations" about the shared personal narratives using questions, comments, and responses that are scaffolded by the conversation facilitator as needed.

If the SLP is to be the conversation partner, the SLP coaches the conversation facilitator on how to prompt responses from the child. Possible prompts include:

- **Verbal cue.** For example, "Ask (conversation partner), 'What happened?'" or "Say, 'I have a dog, too!'"

- **Written cue.** For example, the conversation facilitator hands the child a pre-prepared card on which a question is written and says "Ask (conversation partner) this question." (See Figure 7.2.)

- **Partial cue.** For example, the conversation facilitator provides only the first part of the question or comment and pauses for the child to complete it.

Story Lessons

Conversation Partner's Personal Narrative: Hurt Knee

The conversation partner shows pictures 1 through 4 one at a time.

1	2	3	4
I was walking.	There was a rock on the side walk.	I tripped on the rock!	I fell and hurt my knee!

The conversation facilitator hands a printed question to the child and whispers, "Ask this question."

Child: Was your knee bleeding?

Conversation partner: Yes my knee was bleeding!

The conversation facilitator hands the next question to the child and whispers, "Ask this question."

Child: Did you get a Band-Aid?

The conversation partner shows picture 5: Yes, my friend gave me a Band-Aid.

The conversation facilitator hands the last question to the child and prompts the child to ask it.

Child: Did you feel better?

The conversation partner shows the next picture.

Conversation partner: Yes, my knee felt better!

Note: If the child is a nonreader, the questions may be whispered by the conversation facilitator.

Figure 7.2. A strategy for facilitating conversation using question cards.

Some children in Level II are not yet able to formulate questions like those in the sample exchange above. However, given the familiarity of the topic (hurt knee) and the visual cues in the pictures, they likely understand the gist of them. Although an exchange like this is completely scripted at first, many children enjoy being able to participate in conversation in a new and more competent way.

Over time, the conversation facilitator can sometimes reduce the scaffolding to a partial prompt, "Ask, was your knee _____?" And sometimes after experience with several personal narratives of a similar type (stories about losing something, for example), some children can generate a question like, "Did you find your ...?" without any prompting.

Table 7.7 shows the conversation framework applied at Level II.

Table 7.7
Creating Conversation in Level II

Creating Conversation in Level II	
Exchange greetings	Upon seeing the child at the start of the session, the conversation partner smiles and pauses a moment to let child be the first to greet; if the child does not, the conversation facilitator prompts the child to greet.
Transition to 1st story	The conversation partner makes a leading comment like, "I had a great weekend." or "Something scary/funny happened." Then she pauses for the child to ask a related question; the conversation facilitator may verbally or visually prompt the child's response.
Tell 1st story	After telling the high point of the story (e.g., "I lost my dog!"), the conversation partner pauses to allow time for a response from the child. If the child does not respond, the conversation facilitator provides support to facilitate a response.
Engage in reciprocal exchange about 1st story	At the end of the story, the conversation partner looks expectantly, and pauses for the child to comment or ask a question. If child does not, the conversation facilitator scaffolds a comment or question, and the conversation partner responds.
Transition to 2nd story	The conversation partner looks expectantly and shifts gaze between the child and the child's story pictures to allow the child a chance to initiate his own story. If the child does not initiate, the conversation partner invites the child's story with an animated leading comment like, "You did something ..."
Tell 2nd story	While the child's story is told (with the help of the conversation facilitator as needed), the conversation partner shows attention and interest with body language, facial expressions, "mm-hm's," "oh's," and "wow's." The conversation partner generally does not interrupt the child's story with comments or questions.
Engage in reciprocal exchange about 2nd story	At the end of the child's story, the conversation partner may comment and ask 1-2 questions about the story to which she knows the child can respond. The child responds (with cueing from the conversation partner if needed).

Part 3: Story Practice

If the child has not already done so, the interventionist facilitates independent retelling of the story in the past tense without visual cues after the conversation phase.

Typically, if the child produces errors, the interventionist scaffolds correct language production and invites the child to tell the story again until he can produce it without errors. When the child can produce the story correctly using visual cues, the interventionist encourages him to tell the story again, but this time without pictures. This facilitates the child's ability to both visualize the story and tell it from memory. The story may then be practiced a few times without pictures with help given as needed (e.g., a verbal hint or "picture peek") until the child can independently tell the story correctly in the past tense.

Sometimes a child continues to struggle with a particular sentence form or vocabulary word during Story Practice. When that happens, a Side Lesson is called for to address that item more intensively, as in the following story about Abe.

Abe's Side Lesson: "Take Apart"

Abe was a 12-year-old boy who had significant cognitive and linguistic challenges. He had begun Nurturing Narratives with bare-bones Level I stories but had advanced to Level II stories containing a problem and a solution. With mentoring from Abe's SLP, Abe's mother became very skilled at helping her son prepare personal narratives to tell to his SLP each week. She and Abe co-created his personal narratives as she drew simple stick-figure drawings. Then she helped him practice the stories until he could tell them with a fair amount of independence.

Abe's favorite pastime was to assemble Lego structures. One day he brought a story about a new toy he got for his birthday, called a Motion Power. With the Motion Power, Abe could build motorized Lego vehicles.

Abe's story went like this: "I got a Motion Power. I could not put in a piece. I asked Daddy to help. Daddy put in the piece. I made a helicopter. Daddy put in the batteries. The propeller was spinning. It was cool!"

For a long time, Abe had told his stories in exactly the same words he had practiced with his mother; however, around this time, he had begun to sometimes use his own wording. The day he brought this story, he did something he had never done before – he spontaneously added to the story he had prepared to tell. When he finished talking about the propeller spinning, he tried to say that his father took the helicopter apart and built a car. He said, "Daddy took off the helicopter. He build a car." The sentence "Daddy *took apart* the helicopter." was modeled for him numerous times, but he continued to struggle with how to say *took apart*. Given the importance for Abe of putting together and taking apart Lego structures, his SLP wanted to give him a way to talk about that. She decided to devote their next session to learning *put together* and *take apart*.

The following week, Abe's SLP brought three toys that could be put together and taken apart – a foam glider, a small Lego set, and a simple table-top basketball toy. The same procedure was followed with each toy. Abe was given the toy, asked to put the pieces together, was allowed to play with it for few minutes, and then was asked to take it apart. After that, his SLP helped him create a story – a personal narrative – about the activity. Each story was practiced until Abe could tell it fairly independently; however, he continued to struggle with the construction *take apart*.

Abe was hyperlexic. From a young age, he could decode and "read" quite well, but he had only recently begun to demonstrate some comprehension of what he read. His SLP, wanting to capitalize on this skill, had been using reading and writing as part of Abe's narrative-based language therapy. After they worked on a story about the third toy, she asked Abe to type the story on the computer. When he did so, his SLP saw that he wrote "take a part" instead of "take apart" and she understood the source of his confusion. She then used printed language to help clarify the distinction between the similar sounding word constructions. When he reviewed his three stories for the day, he used the term *take apart* correctly.

Table 7.8 provides an overview of Level II Personal Narratives.

Table 7.8

Overview of Level II Personal Narratives

Level II	Child's and Conversation Partner's Personal Narratives	
Cognitive Complexity	• Story is based on a recent personal experience. • "Causality" is highlighted; most stories contain a simple problem-solution or surprise-consequence. • Visuals (photos, drawings) are used during story telling. • By the end of Level II, child tells story independently in past tense with correct grammar and syntax without visual aids.	
Linguistic Complexity	• Add past tense, compound sentences, and complex sentences with *because*. • May introduce more emotion words and verbs of communication and cognition if the child is ready to understand them.	
Sample Stories	**Child's**	**Adult's**
	1. I was on the swing. I fell down. I was crying. Mom put a Band-Aid on my knee. I felt better. 2. I was playing with my truck. I dropped my truck. I was sad because my truck was broken. Dad fixed my truck. Then I was happy.	1. I had an ice cream cone. I dropped my ice cream. I was sad. (pause) Then I got another ice cream cone, and I was happy. 2. I was playing with my dog. Then my dog ran away! (pause) I was worried. I was yelling my dog's name, "Ellie!" She came back! I was happy because Ellie came back.
Conversation		

- Conversation partner or child initiates exchange of greetings.
- Conversation partner makes a leading comment (e.g., "I had a great weekend." or "Something scary/funny happened to me."), then pauses for child to ask a related question. Conversation facilitator may verbally or visually prompt child's response.
- After telling the high point of story, conversation partner pauses and looks expectantly at child to see if child spontaneously responds. If child does not respond, conversation facilitator provides support to facilitate response.
- After conversation partner's story, conversation facilitator prompts a comment or question from child. Conversation partner responds.
- After onversation partner's story is told, conversation partner "invites" child's story with an animated leading comment like "You did something …"
- At the end of child's story, conversation partner may comment and ask 1-2 questions about story that she knows child can respond to; child responds with cueing from conversation facilitator, if needed.

Level III: Theory of Mind – Sharing Personal Narratives with Low Support and High Demand

Primary Goals for Level III – Sharing Personal Narratives
• Reference to own and others' mental states/perspectives in stories
• Independent retelling of personal narratives with less practice
• Expanded use of complex sentences
• Conversation skills

In Level III, some children may still need to work on complex sentence patterns. For others, their language learning problems involve skills like comprehending abstract vocabulary, organization, and inferencing. At this stage, many demonstrate more difficulty with the social aspects than with the linguistic content of communication.

A primary area of focus in Level III, therefore, is perspective-taking skills. As the conversation facilitator helps the child prepare a personal narrative, and as the child and the conversation partner exchange their personal narratives, there is an emphasis on understanding and talking about the child's and conversation partner's mental states.

Part 1: Story Preparation

In Level III, *c*hildren are usually able to take the lead in creating their own personal narratives. They can determine what experience they want to talk about and what information about it they want to share. But often they still need feedback about the relevance of their utterances to the present situation and help learning how to provide their listeners with enough, but not too much, information.

The conversation facilitator may also offer assistance with organization of the story and suggestions for rewording to express some ideas in complex sentences. Visual supports like drawings may be used to facilitate these skills.

Part 2: Conversation

At this stage, the child has been repeatedly exposed to the conversational framework outlined on page 113. While the conversation partner initiated most aspects of the conversational exchange in the early levels, the child is expected to demonstrate greater initiation and maintenance of conversation in Level III. As the amount of scaffolding is decreased, the child's conversational initiations and responses may be delayed and/or stilted earlier in the level with the goal that they become more fluent later on. See Table 7.9.

Story Lessons

Table 7.9
Creating Conversation: Level III

Creating Conversation in Level III
By Level III, many children are demonstrating some or all of the following skills, but usually not at a level of automaticity. When this is the case, the focus is on refining these conversational skills: • Initiate exchange of greetings • Take the lead in asking for or telling the first story and in facilitating transition from first to second story • Independently respond to the conversation partner's comments and questions about the child's own story • Initiate comments and questions about the conversation partner's story

Part 3: Story Practice

The child may tell his personal narrative using the pictures at first, but then typically retells it without visual aids the second time. The SLP may scaffold corrections either during or following the conversation phase. Table 7.10 gives an overview of Level III personal narratives.

Table 7.10
Overview of Level III Personal Narratives

Level III	Child's and Conversation Partner's Personal Narratives	
Cognitive Complexity	• Story is about a recent personal experience. • Story has a social focus (i.e., reference to own and others' mental states). • Child tells story first with, then without pictures. • By the end of Level III, child is expected to have internalized the framework of the practiced conversational exchange.	
Linguistic Complexity	• Stories contain variety of complex sentences, emotion words, and mental state verbs.	
Sample Stories	**Child's**	**Adult's**
	1. I was at the playground with my brother, Jason. Jason caught a grasshopper but it jumped away. I caught the grasshopper and it sat on my hand a long time. I was happy but Jason was sad. 2. We have a new puppy and her name is Frankie. Frankie stays in the back yard. This morning I looked for Frankie in the back yard but she was gone. The gate was open. I started to cry because I *thought* Frankie was lost. Then Dad came home with Frankie. I was so happy. I was afraid Frankie was lost because I didn't *know* Dad took Frankie for a walk.	Yesterday I lost my keys. I didn't *know* where they were. I looked all over the house but I couldn't *remember* where I put them. I was so frustrated. Then when I was putting on my shoes, I saw my keys. They were under the bed! I *know* I didn't put them there. I *think* maybe my dog put them there! From now on I *think* I will hide my keys in a place where my dog can't find them.

Conversation
• Child initiates exchange of greetings.
• Child takes the lead in asking for or telling the first story, and in facilitating transition from first to second story.
• Child independently responds to the conversation partner's comments and questions about the child's story.
• Child initiates comments and questions about the conversation partner's story.

Segment II: Understanding and Retelling Stories

Story Lessons		
Session Segment	Sharing Personal Narratives	Understanding and Retelling Stories
Story Type	Personal Narratives	Fictional Stories
Description	Child and adult exchange stories about their recent experiences in a conversational context	Story comprehension and retelling are addressed in the context of varied, interactive story repetitions
Key Focus	Expansion of pragmatic skills	Expansion of receptive and expressive language
Similarities	• Top priority: Engagement • Level of story complexity • Focus on mastery of new skills	

During the Understanding and Retelling Stories segment of the Story Lesson, the intent is to continue the warm, interactive connection that was established with the child during Sharing Personal Narratives. The interventionist begins by engaging the child's attention and telling a fictional story that has been "tailored" to facilitate the child's comprehension and interest. Then the interventionist invites the child to join her in telling the story again.

The Four Parts of Understanding and Retelling Stories

Stories are playfully retold several times in different ways, which may include imitating or completing the story sentences, drawing and/or sequencing the story pictures, dictating or typing the story, and/or play-acting a role in the story. The interventionist scaffolds each retelling using evidenced-based techniques to facilitate acquisition of targeted language structures and encourage the child's gradual retelling of more and more of the story on his own. Finally, the child is asked to take the lead in retelling the story and demonstrate the level of "mastery" the SLP has deemed appropriate.

Table 7.11 lists the four parts involved in Understanding and Retelling Stories.

Table 7.11
Four Parts of Understanding and Retelling Stories

Part 1	Story Comprehension
Part 2	Story Practice
Part 3	Best Story!
Part 4	Story Play

Part 1: Story Comprehension

For the most part, a child's personal narratives are meaningful because he had the experience on which they were based. During creation of tailored fictional stories, particular care must be taken to base the story on an event that is familiar to the child and to choose story language that is meaningful to and manageable for the child. Then as the story is told to the child, visual supports are provided to further facilitate story comprehension. Table 7.12 shows options for the child's first exposure to a story.

Table 7.12
Options for First Presentation of the Story

1. Tell the story while acting it out with dolls and toy miniatures.

2. Tell the story while viewing story pictures – pictures are described as they are shown one at a time and then turned face down on the table.

3. Tell the story while viewing the story pictures in a PowerPoint presentation on the computer.

4. Tell the story while looking at story pictures in a book in which the original text is covered if the child can read (sticky notes work well for this).

Concrete language and explicit visual cues are used to support understanding of the earliest Tailored Stories. Then there is a progression toward the use of elaborated text to facilitate story comprehension. Finally, use of visual cues and elaborated text is reduced when the child demonstrates comprehension of stories with less support. The intent is to help the child progress toward comprehension of typical children's story texts.

Table 7.13 demonstrates this general progression; however, in practice, support for comprehension is offered at whatever level is needed regardless of the Level the child is in.

Table 7.13

First Story Presentation Through the Levels

Level I	High level of contextualization (simple, concrete language; story may be acted out with toys; pictures closely match story text) to facilitate story comprehension
Level II	Story pictures less closely match text; elaborated text is used to connect ideas, define new words, and reduce need for inferencing
Level III	Story pictures may minimally match text; thought bubbles in pictures may be used to facilitate comprehension of characters' perspectives; elaborated language is used as needed

Side Lessons

In order for the child to meaningfully retell a story, he must clearly understand the story first. As stories are told and repeated, the interventionist looks for indications of comprehension problems. When a child demonstrates persistent difficulty understanding a sentence pattern, word, or idea in the story, a Side Lesson may be called for. During Side Lessons, the troublesome item is focused on intensively to ensure comprehension. A Side Lesson may last just a few minutes or longer if needed.

On page 123 is the story of a Side Lesson that lasted a whole session to establish one child's comprehension of a single verb. The verb described a key action in the child's favorite play activity, and his SLP thought it was important for him to "own" this word.

Using Questions to Promote Understanding of the Story

Parents, teachers, and SLPs routinely ask questions to assess children's comprehension and knowledge. Questions can also function to highlight important aspects of an event. For example, asking a child at a parade, "Where is the elephant?" suggests to the child that the elephant might be worth paying attention to. In a similar way, questions may be used to direct a child's attention to what is important in a story and, at the same time, facilitate the child's "sense of story."

Understanding question forms and knowing how to respond to them are important skills for children to attain. However, question asking sometimes has negative consequences. Many children with CLP have difficulty fielding questions and may withdraw from interactions if asked too many questions they cannot answer. Research has also shown that young children demonstrate greater gains in language acquisition when their parents use a "responsive" rather than a "directive" style when interacting with them (Mahoney & MacDonald, 2007).

A **responsive style** is characterized by descriptive comments related to the child's focus of interest along with recasts and extensions of the child's utterances; a **directive style** involves frequent questioning and has a "testing" quality to it. While a responsive style of interacting with children is recommended in Nurturing Narratives, we also want to help children develop the ability to understand and respond appropriately to questions. Table 7.14 lists recommendations for addressing both of these goals during story-based intervention.

Table 7.14

Recommendations for Questions

Limit question asking.	Strive for a ratio of 80% comments to 20% questions
Present questions to children in a developmental sequence.	Base earlier questions on concrete "here-and-now" information. Examples include "What is …?" "Who has …?" "What is … doing?" and "Where is …?" Then when these are responded to successfully, introduce "yes/no" questions and questions about the past. Finally, address responding to questions that require reasoning or inferencing.
In the earlier levels, make sure that the information requested in the question is stated in the story.	This is true even for reasoning questions when children are first exposed to them. In the following story excerpt, elaborated language was used to make a casual connection in the story explicit, and thus provide the information needed to answer the question, "Why was the girl mad?" *Sallie was riding her bike. Then her brother took her bike. Sallie was mad because her brother took her bike!*
Ask only questions that facilitate understanding of the story or help the child develop a sense of story.	This practice eliminates many questions that could be asked but that are irrelevant to understanding the story. For example, one would not ask a question about the color of a dog in a story unless that information was needed for comprehension of the story. However, if there were two dogs in the story and one of the dogs did something central to the story, then the color of the dog could be information needed by the listener in order to understand the story.

Table 7.15 lists specific sample questions for each Level of Nurturing Narratives.

Table 7.15

Sample Questions at Each Level of Nurturing Narratives

Level I	Who is ...? What is/are X doing? Which one has ...? Who/Which one can ...? Who likes/wants/needs/feels ...? Where is/are ...?
Level II	What happened? Who wanted, thinks, knows, forgot ...? What did X do? Why did X do Y? How did X feel?
Level III	Where will X look? Where does X think ...? Who knows/doesn't know? How does she know/feel? Why did X do that? Why did X feel ...? What do you think X will do now?

Part 2: Story Practice

To achieve mastery of new skills, children with CLP need repeated practice with learning targets in meaningful contexts. During Understanding and Retelling Stories, the interventionist tells the story to the child first and then scaffolds the child's retelling of the story multiple times with decreasing levels of support.

Mastery of targeted language skills and story retelling is facilitated with evidence-based techniques (see Appendix F). The goal is to gradually "hand over" the telling of the story to the child. In order to maintain the child's attention and interest, deepen the child's grasp of new skills, and solidify ownership of the story, it is important to vary the ways in which stories are retold.

Story Practice
The goal of repeated and varied practice of stories is to create a story-centered context in which the child and interventionist interact and have fun together while story comprehension is solidified, language patterns are practiced, and memory of the story is facilitated.

Story Lessons

Options for Repeated Story Practice

1. **Story sentence imitation** – Invite the child to repeat sentences after the interventionist models them.

2. **Sentence completion** – Begin the sentences and pause for the child to complete them.

3. **Comprehension questions** – During retelling of the story, ask questions about the story that are appropriate for the child's developmental level.

4. **Sequencing the story pictures** – "Accidentally" drop the pictures and ask the child to "fix" them.

5. **Picture description** – Invite the child to tell the story while looking at the story pictures with one in view at a time; offer support as needed using recasts, expansions, and so on.

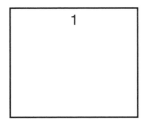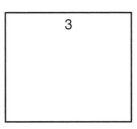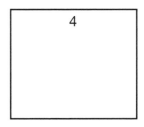

6. **Acting out the story with toys** – Ask the child to "narrate" the story while he or the interventionist manipulates the toys.

7. **Stickwriting** (Ukrainetz, 1998) – Draw quick impressionistic sketches to represent the story ideas. This is something akin to writing story notes; it should take no longer to draw a sketch than it would take to jot down a word. In this way, the child's memory is aided, but the flow of telling the story is not disrupted while detailed pictures are drawn.

I had some flowers. I got some water and I poured water on the flowers.

Uh oh, I spilled water on the table. I got a towel and wiped the table. Then the table was dry.

8. **Drawing** – Ask the child if he wants to draw the story pictures; while or after they are drawn, ask the child to tell the story. For some children, drawing is grounding and organizing.

| Here are some ladies. They have hats. The wind is blowing. | The hats blew away! The ladies are sad! |

9. **Drawing from the child's dictation** – Say you want to draw the pictures and ask the child to "tell me" or "help me remember" what to draw; alternatively, the SLP and child can draw simultaneously while talking about what to draw.

10. **Typing or writing from the child's dictation** – Ask the child what to say as you write the text on the pictures one of you has drawn or as you type the story on the computer. Many children like to dictate the sentences to be typed in "text boxes" under the story pictures, which have been scanned and inserted into a PowerPoint presentation.

11. **Tape recording** – Tell the child his story is so great you want to record it.

12. **Video** – Again, praise the child for telling such a great story and ask if you can make a movie of it.

13. **Reading** – If the child reads, ask the child to read the story text aloud.

14. **Reading word cards** – Write key words, especially those that cannot be pictured like *but* and *because,* on cards to facilitate the child's memory and production of them.

15. **Writing** – Ask the child to write or type the story on the computer either in a Word document or a PowerPoint presentation in which the story pictures have been inserted.

16. Reading/writing – Ask the child to complete a "story guide," a printed version of the story in which some words or phrases are replaced with blanks which the child fills in.

The following two strategies may be used with children who are able to think more abstractly.

17. Visual representation of detailed versus summarized story retelling – Tell the child, "You gave me all the details in the story like this …"

"I only need to know what it is mostly about. Tell the story this way …"

18. **Story Grammar Marker**® (Moreau & Fidrych, 2008) – Introduce children to the abstract concept of story grammar using Braidy the StoryBraid® or the Story Grammar Marker® from MindWing Concepts, Inc. (see Figure 7.3). These hands-on tools contain icons that represent the different components of story grammar (character, setting, initiating event, etc.) and offer a visual, kinesthetic representation of the developmental sequence of a story episode.

Figure 7.3. **Braidy the StoryBraid**® **and Story Grammar Marker.**®
Pictures used with permission from MindWing Concepts, Inc.

How Many Story Repetitions?

The number of times a story is repeated depends on the child. Some children want to move on to something new after a story has been reviewed only two or three times. Particularly in the early stages of Nurturing Narratives, that wish is generally honored, and a new story is presented if that is what is needed to keep the interaction positive and the child engaged. However, once children become familiar with and begin to experience some success during the story-based activities, they are often willing to repeat a story multiple times. As children progress through the Levels, there is a general expectation that they will be able to "master" stories with fewer and fewer rounds of practice.

Story Practice Routines of Two SLPs

The choice of story practice strategies varies according to the interventionist and the child. Below are examples of the typical "routines" used by two therapists. Throughout their sessions, these SLPs use evidence-based language facilitation techniques to respond to errors and address the child's language goals.

Story Lessons

Emily's Story Practice Routine

Emily often tells a story first as she acts it out with toys in order to engage children and help them create a mental movie of the story. Before telling a story a second time, she says, "Let's tell the story together!" She reenacts the story while eliciting the child's imitation of each story sentence. (If the child wants to manipulate the toys (most do), Emily may say something like, "I'll do the toys now and you can do them next time.") For the third retelling she may say, "Help me tell the story this time." She then begins each sentence and pauses to let the child complete it. For the fourth round, she may offer one of the toys to the child, "Do you want to drive the car?!" or give all of the toys either saying, "You do the toys and I'll tell the story." (she watches to see if the child matches the actions of the toys to the story language), or asking "Can you tell the story?" to see how the child does independently. If the child seems reluctant, Emily says, "Let's tell it together." or "I can help you." When the child makes errors, she generally responds to them with "recasts" of the child's utterances.

Emily may then suggest they draw pictures of the story. She whisks away the toys and brings out index cards and markers. Some children want to draw; others don't. Emily encourages the child to remember the story by asking, "What happened first?" or "What should I draw?" Or she just starts the first sentence, "Here … is …a …," pausing to see if and when the child can chime in. If the child wants to draw, she asks the child to tell what he is going to draw before starting each picture. (Note: Having the child draw sometimes helps the child slow down, focus, and organize his language. At other times, drawing can be distracting and disorganizing if, for example, the child gets overly excited, loses track of the story, or wants to change it.)

When the story pictures are drawn, Emily may "accidentally" drop them and ask the child to "fix" them. Once the pictures are sequenced, she may address answering questions about the story. She will also use the pictures to work on solidifying the challenging sentence pattern(s) in the story. With each repetition of the story, she scaffolds the child's retelling of more and more of the story on his own.

Neisha's Story Practice Routine

Neisha prefers to tell the story first using story pictures that have been scanned and placed in a PowerPoint presentation. She sets the slide size to fill the screen and tells the story as she shows each picture. Many children enjoy pressing the key on the computer to advance the pictures. Neisha repeats the story on the computer two or three more times as she addresses sentence imitation, sentence completion, picture description, and question answering. She may ask the child to dictate the story to her so she can type the text in text boxes under the pictures on the slides. Alternatively, children who can type might insert the text themselves, verbalizing each sentence before typing it. Neisha attempts to elicit most of the story practice using pictures on the computer.

Next, they move away from the computer, and Neisha asks the child to select from a basket the toys needed for the story. She and the child interactively retell the story as they act it out with toys. Finally, Neisha prints out the story picture slides (as handouts, with two slides per page), and asks the child to retell the story while referencing the pictures. When the child seems ready, Neisha says it is time for him to be the "best story teller" and elicits the child's final retelling of the story.

Emily's routine might be appropriate for a younger or lower functioning child who needs to see the story sequence unfold in more detail than can be offered in pictures. Introducing a story with toys might also be more effective with a child who is difficult to engage. However, toys can distract some children and interfere with language comprehension and production. These children often perform better when the story is practiced first with pictures, and acting it out with toys is the reward. Interventionists are encouraged to experiment with different story practice strategies and use those that work best to retain the child's attention, engagement and intensive practice of therapy goals.

Table 7.17 overviews the story practice routines used by Emily and Neisha.

Table 7.17

Samples of Story Practice Routines

	Emily's Routine **Story presentation with toys**	**Neisha's Routine** **Story presentation with pictures scanned into a PowerPoint presentation**
1	Story repeated while acting it out with toys: • Sentence imitation	Story repeated on computer: • Sentence imitation
2	• Sentence completion	• Sentence completion
3	• Child acts out story with toys as interventionist tells the story	• Child describes story pictures
4	• Child tells story while acting it out with toys	• Child dictates story while interventionist or child types in text under pictures
5	Interactive retelling of story while drawing story pictures	• Child dictates story while interventionist or child types in text under pictures
6	Child sequences story pictures	Child selects story toys from toy basket
7	Child describes story pictures	Interactive story retelling while acting story out with toy miniatures
8	Question answering (using pictures)	Child sequences story pictures (slides printed 2-4 to a page)
9	Child retells story (with or without story pictures)	Child retells the story (with or without story pictures)

Part 3: Best Story!

Once a story has been practiced several times with scaffolded support, and when the child seems ready, it is time for the final story retelling; this is a higher demand/lower support situation. The criteria for the final story retelling differ, depending on the Level the child is in and the goals the SLP is targeting for the child. Like stories, story retelling expectations are "tailored" to the child.

The final story retelling is set apart from story practice. Interventionists use different ways of setting it up with children. For example, one SLP says, "Okay, now it is time for you to be the best story teller!" Another may ask a child in Level II or III, "Can you tell the story now with *no pictures*?!?"

Regardless of how the final story retelling is introduced, the message to the child is that this is a big deal – a moment for the child to shine. Without saying it in these words, the SLP communicates that "It will be a challenge, but I believe you can do it!" Excitement is conveyed at the prospect of witnessing this wonderful performance.

The SLP has predetermined the level of story retelling she thinks the child is capable of producing independently. The child may not reach that on the first try, and the SLP might need to help with some prompting. The SLP will determine how many retellings to ask for. Some children seem discouraged if asked to repeat the story more than a couple of times; others are motivated to "beat" their past performance and will try several times. Ideally, the challenge is one the child can meet with some effort. The SLP's feedback should be honest; praise should not be empty. The therapist might say something like, "That was a good story, but I helped you just a little." followed up with, "Can you tell the story *all by yourself*?!?"

When the story retelling does meet the criteria for the child's "best story," especially when the child "stretched" to do it," praise should be lavish. "That was your best story! You are a great story teller!" or "You are the best story teller!" And while the child is feeling good about his accomplishment, it might be an opportune time to suggest retelling it to someone else so the child gets even more practice and demonstrates his competence again. "I bet Mom (or someone else) would love this story. Let's tell it to her!"

Table 7.18 lists the expectations for Best Story retelling at each level.

Table 7.18

Expectation for "Best Story" Retelling at Each Level

Level I – Events		Level II – Surprises		Level III – Theory of Mind	
Early	Late	Early	Late	Early	Late
• Interactive retelling of stories with visual and verbal cueing • Story toys or pictures are used as memory cues	• Interactive retelling of stories • Begin to practice re-telling stories without the pictures after story practice with them	• Retelling of stories with minimal visual or verbal cue-ing	• Independent retelling of stories with-out visual or verbal cueing	• Independent retelling of stories with-out visual or verbal cueing	• Independent retelling of stories with-out visual or verbal cueing

Part 4: Story Play

Once a child has "mastered" a story, he may be ready to take it to a new level – pretend play. During Story Play, the child and interventionist or child and peers take on the roles of the story characters and act them out. The story may be acted out using the story toys or in role-plays.

Table 7.19 lists suggested story play activities.

Story Lessons

Table 7.19

Story Play Activities

Play Preparation
• When presented with a basket of various toys, the child chooses those needed for the story. Higher functioning children may be asked to tell why they did/did not choose a particular toy. -or- Ask the child to recall the toys needed, "What do we need for our story?"   • Facilitate problem solving and planning – Ask the child to think about the props needed to role-play the story, "What could we use for an ice cream cone?" "How can we make a car?"   • Negotiate roles, "Who do you want to be?" "Do you want to be Big Al or a little fish?" "Can I be the dad first? Next time you could be the dad."
Acting
• The child and interventionist or peer(s) each take on the role of a story character as the story is acted out with toys or as it is role-played with props.   • The story can be acted out a second time with roles reversed and possibly more times with negotiated revisions or elaborations to the text.
Benefits of Story Play
• Development of pretend play skills   • Flexibility with language as the story text is altered to reflect the interaction being portrayed (e.g., "I want some pizza." or "May I have some pizza?" versus "The boy wants some pizza.").   • Opportunities for cooperation, collaboration, and negotiation   • Learning about others' perspectives as character roles are exchanged   • Opportunity to develop play routines and story scripts that can be used in play with peers

Table 7.20 discusses story play through the Levels.

Table 7.20

Story Play Through the Levels

STORY PLAY THROUGH THE LEVELS
Story Theme
The stories that are play-acted increase in complexity through the Levels. Level I stories are based on short, simple routines or events while Level II stories have a problem and solution. In Level III, there is a focus on expressing characters' internal reactions to problems, plans for resolving the problems and so on.
Story Props
As children move through the Levels it is expected that they will be able to use props that are less concrete and more representational. Some children will be able to use imaginary props.
Story Planning
As children progress through the Levels, they are also offered opportunities to take more of a lead in planning the story play and initiating negotiations regarding what props to use or make, who will play which character and so on.

Story Lessons with Groups in a School Setting

The decision to conduct story lessons in individual or group sessions is based on the needs of the child. Individual therapy can promote establishment of foundation skills such as attention, motivation and reciprocal interactions with adults. Group therapy allows for peer modeling, generalization of skills, and promotion of communication skills with peers. More about using Nurturing Narratives with groups may be found in Appendix D.

Chapter 8

Nurturing Narratives: Simplify and Support, Play and Practice

Two Stories About "Not"

At the beginning of this book, we told some stories about a boy named Pete, his mom, Alice, and his SLP, Kate. It seems fitting to circle back and close with a couple more stories about them.

Comparing Two Restaurants

Pete had particular difficulty learning to express negation with "not." Kate and Alice had tried to teach Pete the meaning of "not" through numerous activities and stories, but nothing seemed to work. Then one day, during a discussion with Alice about Pete's event knowledge, Kate got an idea for a side lesson which might help.

Alice told Kate that one topic Pete knew a lot about was restaurants. Alice said that she and her husband worked all week at their jobs and did not want to cook on weekends, so the family ate out every Friday and Saturday night. Alice reported that Pete knew which restaurants had which foods, which had children's menus, and so on.

Kate asked Alice to help Pete prepare a "report" comparing two restaurants to bring to his next session. This activity lent itself to working not only on "not," but also production of compound sentences containing "but," which was another of Pete's treatment goals.

At the next session, Pete arrived with some simple pictures that his mother had drawn for him to use as a visual reference. Pete seemed anxious to begin so Kate asked him what he wanted to tell her. Pete sat up straight and told the following **with authority**!

I like to eat at Marie Callender's, and I like to eat at Sushi Boat.

Marie Callender's has Fettuccini Alfredo, **but** Sushi Boat does not have Fettuccini Alfredo.

Marie Callendar's has coloring and kid's menu, **but** Sushi Boat does not have coloring and kid's menu.

Marie Callendar's has vanilla ice cream, **but** Sushi Boat does not have vanilla ice cream.

Marie Callendar's has lemon pie, **but** Sushi Boat does not have lemon pie.

Sushi Boat has tofu skin, **but** Marie Callendar's does not have tofu skin.

Sushi Boat has boats. Marie Callendar's does not have boats.

Sushi Boat has green tea. Marie Callendar's does not have green tea.

Sushi Boat has rice and fish, **but** Marie Callendar's does not have fish and rice.

The task was so challenging that Pete sometimes omitted regular plurals, but Kate hardly cared about that! Pete had done a fantastic job, and when he finished his report, he looked extremely proud of himself.

"Not My Pants"

A few weeks later, Alice called Kate to tell her another story about "not." She said that the day before she had been doing the dishes in the kitchen when she realized Pete was saying something over and over in the next room. When she went to investigate, she saw that Pete's dad was folding laundry, and Pete was helping him put the clothes away. Apparently, Pete's dad had mistakenly handed Pete his sister's pants and told Pete to put them in his drawer. Pete was holding up the pants and telling his dad, "Not my pants." It seems Pete finally *had* "not."

It All Comes Back to the "Tricky Mix"

In Chapter 2, we quoted Nelson et al. (2001), who wrote, "Successful learning … always involves what we term a Tricky Mix of multiple, positive, and converging cognitive, communicative, social, emotional, and self-esteem factors" (p. 159). In working with children with CLP, we find it to be true that determining the right mix of factors to create successful learning is often indeed "tricky," especially for children who are lower functioning. The stories in this book about Pete and many other children attest to that! Yet, those same stories also demonstrate that meaningful gains in language skills can be facilitated for those children.

There is no one way to create the right Tricky Mix; however, we continue to find the **"4 M's,"** the principles of the Nurturing Narratives approach, to be significant factors in our successful intervention with children. And so, we will leave you with the suggestion to …

- **mentor** the children you work with and key adults in their lives well,

- keep adapting stories and other learning material until they are **meaningful** and **manageable**, and

- create opportunities for reaching **mastery** of new skills through intensive scaffolded practice,

… to facilitate the right Tricky Mix for language learning!

An Invitation

We would love to hear about your experiences with Nurturing Narratives story-based intervention and invite you to share your favorite Tailored Stories and Story Lesson success stories with us. We can be contacted at nurturingnarratives@coachingcomprehension.com.

References

Arwood, E. L., Kaulitz, C., & Brown, M. (2009). *Visual thinking strategies for individuals with autism spectrum disorders: The language of pictures.* Shawnee Mission, KS: Autism Asperger Publishing Company.

Arwood, E. L., & Kaulitz, C. (2007). *Learning with a visual brain in an auditory world.* Shawnee Mission, KS: Autism Asperger Publishing Company.

Astington, J. W. (2001). The future of theory-of-mind research: understanding motivational states, the role of language, and real-world consequences. *Child Development, 72,* 685-687.

Astington, J. W., & Jenkins, J. M. (1999). A longitudinal study of the relation between language and theory of mind development. *Developmental Psychology, 35,* 1311-1320.

Baer, D., Wolf, M., & Risley, R. (1968). Some current dimensions of applied behavior analysis. *Journal of Applied Behavior Analysis, 1,* 91-97.

Baron-Cohen, S. (1995). *Mindblindness: An essay on autism and theory of mind.* Cambridge, MA: MIT Press/Bradford Books.

Baron-Cohen, S., Leslie, A. M., & Frith, U. (1985). Does the autistic child have a "theory of mind"? *Cognition, 21,* 37-46.

Beck, I. L., McKeown, M. G., Omanson, R. C., & Pople, M. J. (1984). Improving the comprehensibility of stories: The effects of revisions that improve coherence. *Reading Research* Quarterly, *19*(3), 263-277.

Beukelman, D. R., & Mirenda, P. (1998). *Augmentative and alternative communication: Management of severe communication disorders in children and adults* (2nd ed.). Baltimore: Paul H. Brookes Publishing Co.

Bishop, D.V.M., & Edmundson, A. (1987). Language impaired 4-year-olds: Distinguishing transient from persistent impairment. *Journal of Speech and Hearing Disorders, 52,* 156-173.

Blank, M. (2002). Classroom discourse: A key to literacy. In K. Butler & E. Silliman (Eds.), *Speaking, reading and writing in children with learning disabilities: New paradigms in research and practice* (pp. 151-173). Malwah, NJ: Erlbaum.

Blank, M., Marquis, A., & Klimovitch, M. (1995). *Directing early school discourse.* Tucson, AZ: Communication Skill Builders a division of The Psychological Corporation.

Blank, M., Rose, S., & Berlin, L. (2003). *Preschool language assessment instrument-2* (PLAI-2). Austin, TX: Pro-Ed, Inc.

Botting, N., Faragher, B., Knox, E., Simkin, Z. & Conti-Ramsden, G. (2001). Predicting pathways of SLI: What differentiates the best and the worst outcomes. *Journal of Child Psychology & Psychiatry, 42*(8), 1013-1020.

Brown, A. L., & Reeve, R. A. (1987). Bandwidths of competence: The role of supportive contexts in learning and development. In L. S. Liben (Ed.), *Development and learning: Conflict or congruence* (pp.173-223). Hillsdale. NJ: Lawrence Erlbaum Associates Inc.

Buehl, D. (2001). *Classroom strategies for interactive learning* (2nd ed.). Newark, DE: International Reading Association.

Camarata, S., Nelson, K., & Camarata, M. (1994). Comparison of conversational recast and imitative procedures for training grammatical structures in children with developmental delay. *Journal of Speech, Language and Hearing Research, 37,* 1414-1423.

Chong, I. M., & Carr, J. E. (2005). An investigation of the potentially adverse effects of task interspersal, *Behavioral Interventions, 20*(4), 285-300.

Connell, P., & Stone, A. (1992). Morpheme learning of children with specific language impairment under controlled instructional conditions. *Journal of Speech, Language, and Hearing Research, 35,* 844-852.

Corrigan, R. (2008). Beyond the obvious: Constructing meaning from subtle patterns in the language environment. *Communication Disorders Quarterly, 29,* 109-124.

Cousins, L. (1999). *Maisy's bedtime.* Somerville, MA: Candlewick.

Cowley, J. (1999). *Mrs. Wishy-Washy.* New York: Philomel Books, A Division of Penguin Putman Books for Young Readers.

Coxe, M (1996). *Cat traps.* New York: Random House Children's Books.

Cross, T. (1977). Mothers' speech adjustments: The contribution of selected child listener variables. In C. Snow & C. Ferguson (Eds.), *Talking to children* (pp. 151-188). London: Cambridge University Press.

Culatta, B. (1994). Representation play and story enactments: Formats for language intervention. In J. Duchan, L. Hewitt, & R. Sonnenmeier (Eds.), *Pragmatics: From theory to practice* (pp. 105-119). Englewood Cliffs, NJ: Prentice Hall.

Dawson, J. I., Stout, C. E., & Eyer, J. A. (2003). *Structured photographic expressive language test: Third edition (SPELT-3).* DeKalb, IL: Janelle Publications.

References

Donaldson, M. L., Reid, J., & Murray, C. (2007). Causal sentence production in children with language impairments. *International Journal of Language & Communication Disorders, 42*(2), 155-186.

Duchan, J. F. (1997). A situated pragmatics approach for supporting children with severe communication disorders. *Topics in Language Disorders, 17*(2), 1-18.

Dunlap, G., & Koegel, R. L. (1980). Motivating autistic children through stimulus variation. *Journal of Applied Behavior Analysis, 13*, 619-627.

Dunn, L. M., & Dunn, D. M. (2007). *Peabody picture vocabulary test* (4th ed.). Upper Saddle River, NJ: Pearson.

Engel, S. (1999). *The stories children tell*. New York: W. H. Freeman & Co.

Evans, D. D., & Strong, C. J. (1996). What's the story? *Teaching Exceptional Children, 96*(28), 25-62.

Fenson, L., Marchman, V. A., Thal, D. J., Dale, P. S., Reznick, J. S., & Bates, E. (2007). *Mac-Arthur-Bates communicative development inventories: User's guide and technical manual* (2nd ed.). Baltimore: Paul H. Brookes Publishing Co.

Fey, M. E. (1986). *Language intervention with young children*. Boston: Allyn & Bacon.

Fey, M. E., Cleave, P. L., Long, S. H., & Hughes, D. L. (1993). Two approaches to the facilitation of grammar in language-impaired children: An experimental evaluation. *Journal of Speech and Hearing Research, 36*, 141-157.

Ford, J. A., & Milosky, L. M. (2003). Inferring emotional reactions in social situations: differences in children with specific language impairment. *Journal of Speech, Language, and Hearing Research, 46*, 21-30.

Goodman, G., Duchan, J., & Sonnenmeier, R. (1994). Children's development of scriptal knowledge. In J. Duchan, L. Hewitt, & R. Sonnenmeier (Eds.), *Pragmatics: From theory to practice* (pp.120-133). Englewood Cliffs, NJ: Prentice-Hall.

Greenspan, S., & Lewis, D. (2005). *The affect-based language curriculum (ablc) an intensive program for families, therapists and teachers* (2nd ed.). Baltimore: Interdisciplinary Council on Developmental and Learning Disorders.

Greenspan, S., & Weider, S. (2006). *Engaging autism: Helping children relate, communicate and think with the DIR Floortime Approach*. New York: DeCapo Press.

Greenwood, C. R., Walker, H. M., Todd, N. M., & Hops, H. (1981). Normative and descriptive analysis of preschool free play social interaction rates. *Journal of Pediatric Psychology, 6*, 343-367.

Gutstein, S., & Sheely, R. (2002). *Relationship development intervention with young children*. London & Philadelphia: Jessica Kingsley Publishers Ltd.

Hadley, P. A., & Rice, M. L. (1991). Conversational responsiveness of speech-impaired and language-impaired preschoolers. *Journal of Speech and Hearing Research, 34*(6), 1308-1317.

Hardy, B. (1977). Narrative as a primary act of mind. In M. Meek, A. Warlow & G. Barton (Eds.), *The cool web; The pattern of children's reading* (pp.12-23). London: Bodley Head.

Hayward, D., & Schneider, P. (2000). Effectiveness of teaching story grammar knowledge to preschool children with language impairment: An exploratory study. *Child Language Teaching and Therapy*, 255-284.

Healy, J. (1999). *Endangered minds: Why children don't think and what we can do about it.* New York: Touchstone Books.

Hedberg, N., & Westby, C. (1993). *Analyzing story-telling skills: Theory to practice.* Tucson, AZ: Communication Skill Builders.

Hedge, M., & Maul, C. (2006). *Language disorders in children: An evidence-based approach to assessment and treatment.* Boston: Pearson.

Howlin, P., Baron-Cohen, S., & Hadwin, J. (1999). *Teaching children with autism to mind-read: A practical guide for teachers and parents.* West Sussex, England: Wiley.

Hudson, J. (2004). The development of future thinking: constructing future events in mother-child conversation. In J. Lucariello, J. Hudson, R. Fivish, & P. Bauer (Eds.), *The development of the mediated mind: Sociocultural context and cognitive development* (pp. 127-150). Hillsdale, NJ: Lawrence Erlbaum Associates.

Hudson, J. A., & Shapiro, L. R. (1991). From knowing to telling: The development of children's scripts, stories, and personal narratives. In A. McCabe & C. Peterson (Eds.), *Developing narrative structure* (pp. 89-136). Hillsdale, NJ: Lawrence Erlbaum Associates.

Ingersoll, B. (2010). Teaching social communication: A comparison of naturalistic behavioral and developmental, social-pragmatic approaches for children with autism spectrum disorders. *Journal of Positive Behavior Interventions, 12,* 33-43.

Johnston, J. (2006). *Thinking about child language.* Eau Claire, WI: Thinking Publications.

Just, M. A., & Carpenter, P. A. (1992). A capacity theory of comprehension: Individual differences in working memory. *Psychological Review, 98,* 122-149.

Kaderavek, J. N., & Hunt, A. (2005). *Evidence-based practice for narrative interventions: beyond sequence pictures.* Paper presented at the ASHA Convention, San Diego, CA.

Kaderavek, J. N., & Rabidoux, P. (2004). Interactive to independent literacy: A model for designing literacy goals for children with atypical communication. *Reading & Writing Quarterly, 20,* 237-260.

References

Kaufman, A., & Kaufman, N. (2004). *Kaufman assessment battery for children* (2nd ed.). Menlo Park, CA: Pearson Assessments.

Kirchner, D. (1991). Using verbal scaffolding to facilitate conversational participation and language acquisition in children with pervasive developmental disorders. *Journal of Childhood Communication Disorders, 14*, 81-96.

Kirchner, D. M. (1991). Reciprocal book reading: A discourse based intervention strategy for the child with atypical language development. In T. M. Gallagher (Ed.), *Pragmatics of language: Clinical practices issues* (pp. 307-332). San Diego, CA: Singular.

Kispal, A. (2008). *Effective teaching of inference skills for reading: Literature review* (DCSF Research Report 031). London: DCSF.

Klecan-Aker, J. (1993). A treatment program for improving story-telling ability: A case study. *Child Language Teaching and Therapy*, 105-113.

Koegel, L. K., & Koegel, R. L. (1986). The effects of interspersed maintenance on academic performance and motivation in a severe childhood stroke victim. *Journal of Applied Behavior Analysis, 19*, 425-430.

Lahey, M., & Bloom, L. (1994). Variability and language learning disabilities. In G. Wallach & K. Butler (Eds.), *Language learning disabilities in school-age children and adolescents* (pp. 354-372). New York: Macmillan.

Le Guin, U. (1989). *Dancing at the edge of the world: Thoughts on words, women, places.* London: Paladin.

Leonard, L. (1998). *Children with specific language impairment.* Cambridge, MA: MIT Press.

Lyle, S. (2000). Narrative understanding: Developing a theoretical context for understanding how children make meaning in classroom settings *Journal of Curriculum Studies, 1*(2), 45-63.

MacDonald, J. D. (1989). *Becoming partners with children: From play to conversation.* San Antonio, TX: Special Press.

Mahoney, G., & MacDonald, J. (2007). *Autism and developmental delays in young children: the responsive teaching curriculum for parents and professionals.* Austin, TX: Pro-Ed.

Mahoney, G., & Perales, F. (2003). Using relationship-focused intervention to enhance the social-emotional functioning of young children with autism spectrum disorders. *Topics in Early Childhood Special Education, 23*, 77-89.

McCabe, A., & Rollins, P. R. (1994). Assessment of preschool narrative skills. *American Journal of Speech-Language Pathology, 3*, 45-56.

McCauley, R., & Fey, M. (Eds.). (2006). *Treatment of language disorders in children.* Baltimore: Paul H. Brookes Publishing Co.

Millward, C., Powell, S., Messer, D., & Jordan, R. (2000). Recall for self and other in autism: Children's memory for events experienced by themselves and their peers. *Journal of Autism and Developmental Disorders, 30*(1), 15-28.

Miranda, A., McCabe, A., & Bliss, L. (1998). Jumping around and leaving things out: A profile of the narrative abilities of children with specific language impairment. *Applied Psycholinguistics, 19*, 647-667.

Montgomery, J. (2008). *Montgomery assessment of vocabulary acquisition*. Greenville, SC: Super Duper Publications. Montgomery, J. (2009). Complex sentence comprehension and working memory in children with specific language impairment. *Journal of Speech, Language, and Hearing Research, 52*, 269-288.

Montgomery, J. (2009). Working memory and comprehension in children with specific language impairment: What we know so far. *Journal of Communication Disorders, 36*, 221-231.

Moreau, M. R., & Fidrych, H. (2002). *How to use the Story Grammar Marker® – A guide for improving speaking, reading and writing skills within your existing program.* Springfield, MA: MindWing Concepts.

Moreau, M. R., & Fidrych, H. (2008). *The Story Grammar Marker® – Teacher's manual.* Springfield, MA: MindWing Concepts.

Morrow, L. M. (1985). Retelling stories: A strategy for improving young children's comprehension, concept of story structure, and oral language complexity. *The Elementary School Journal, 85*(5), 647-661.

Naremore, R., Densmore, A., & Harmon, D. (2001). *Language intervention with school-aged children: Conversation, narrative and text.* San Diego, CA: Singular Publishing.

Nelson K. (1986). *Event knowledge: Structure and function in development*. Hillsdale, NJ: Erlbaum.

Nelson, K. (1996). *Language in cognitive development: Emergence of the mediated mind*. Cambridge; New York: Cambridge University Press.

Nelson, K., & Gruendel, J. (1986). Generalized event representations: Basic building blocks of cognitive development. In A. Brown & M. Lamb (Eds.), *Advances in developmental psychology* (Vol. 1). Hillsdale, NJ: Lawrence Erlbaum Associates.

Nelson, K. E., Craven, P. L., Xuan, Y., & Arkenberg, M. E. (2004). Acquiring art, spoken language, sign language, text, and other symbolic systems: Developmental and evolutionary observations from a dynamic tricky mix theoretical perspective. In J. M. Lucariello, J. A. Hudson, R. Fivush, & P. J. Bauer (Eds.), *The development of the mediated mind* (pp. 175-222). Mahwah, NJ: Lawrence Erlbaum Associates. Nelson, K. E., Welsh, J., Camarata, S., Heimann, & Tjus, T. (2001). A rare event transactional

References

dynamic model of tricky mix conditions contributing to language acquisition and varied communicative delays. In K. E. Nelson, A. Koc, & C. Johnson (Eds.), *Children's language* (Vol. 11). Hillsdale, NJ: Lawrence Erlbaum Associates.

Newcomer, P., & Hammill, D. (2008). *Test of language development-Primary* (4th ed.). Austin, TX: Pro-Ed.

Norris, J., & Hoffman, P. (1993). *Whole language intervention for school-age children*. San Diego, CA: Singular Publishing.

O'Connor, R. E., Notari-Syverson, N., & Vadasy, P. (2005). *Ladders to literacy: A kindergarten activity book*. Baltimore: Paul H. Brookes Publishing Co.

Paley, V. G. (1990). *The boy who would be a helicopter: The uses of storytelling in the kindergarten.* Cambridge, MA: Harvard University Press.

Paul, R. (2007). *Language disorders from infancy through adolescence: Assessment and Intervention* (3rd ed.). St. Louis, MO: Mosby.

Pearson, D. W. (1988). A group therapy idea for new clinicians in the school setting: Keep little hands busy. *Language Speech and Hearing Services in the Schools, 19,* 432.

Pelletier, J., & Astington, J. W. (2004). Action, consciousness and theory of mind: Children's ability to coordinate story characters' actions and thoughts. *Early Education and Development, 15,* 5-22.

Pepper, J., & Weitzman, L. (2004). *It takes two to talk: A practical guide for parents of children with language delays* (3rd ed.). Toronto, ONT: Hanen Centre.

Petersen, D. B. (2010). A systematic review of narrative based language intervention with children who have language impairment. *Communication Disorders Quarterly*. OnlineFirst, published January 13, 2010. doi:10.1177/1525740109353937

Prizant, B., Wetherby, A. M., Rubin, E., Laurent, A., & Rydell, P. (2006). *The SCERTS model. A comprehensive educational approach for children with autism spectrum disorders: Volume II program planning and intervention*. Baltimore: Brookes Publishing.

Renfrew, C. E. (1997). *The Renfrew language scales: Bus story test.* Oxon, UK: Speechmark Publishing Ltd.

Reilly, J., Losh, M., Bellugi, U., & Wulfeck, B. (2004). "Frog, where are you?": Narratives in children with specific language impairment, early focal brain injury and Williams syndrome. *Brain and Language, 88,* 22-247.

Sackett, D. L., Straus, S. E., Richardson, W. S., Rosenberg, W., & Haynes, R. B. (2000). *Evidence-based medicine: How to practice and teach EBM.* Edinburgh, United Kingdom: Churchill Livingstone.

Seymour, H. N., Roeper, T., & de Villiers, J. G. (2005). *Diagnostic evaluation of language variation) norm-referenced test (*DELV-NR). San Antonio, TX: The Psychological Corporation.

Snow, C. E., Perlmann, R., & Nathan, D. (1987). Why routines are different: Toward a multiple-factors model of the relation between input and language acquisition. In K. Nelson & A. van Kleeck (Eds.), *Children's language: Volume 6* (pp. 65-97). Hillsdale, NJ: Lawrence Erlbaum Associates.

Snyder-McLean, L., Solomonson, B., McLean, J., & Sack, S. (1984). Structuring joint action routines: A strategy for facilitating communication and language development in the classroom. *Seminars in Speech and Language, 5*(3), 213-228.

Spackman, M. P., Fujiki, M., & Brinton, H. (2006). Understanding emotions in context: The effects of specific language impairment on children's emotion understanding. *International Journal of Language and Communication Disorders, 41*, 173-188.

Stein, N. L., & Glenn, C. (1979). An analysis of story comprehension in elementary school children. In R. O. Freedle (Ed.), *New directions in discourse processing* (Vol. 2, pp. 53-120). Norwood, NJ: Ablex

Sussman, F. (1999). *More than words: A guide to helping parents promote communication and social skills in children with autism spectrum disorder.* Toronto, ONT: Hanen Centre.

Swanson, L. A., Fey, M. E, & Mills, C. (2005). Use of narrative-based language intervention with children who have specific language impairment. *American Journal of Speech Language Pathology, 14*(2), 131-143.

Tager-Flusberg, H., & Sullivan, K. (1994). Predicting and explaining behavior: A comparison of autistic, mentally retarded and normal children. *Journal of Child Psychology and Psychiatry, 35*(6), 1059-1075.

Taubman, M., Brierly, S., Wisher, J., Baker, D., McEachin, J., & Leaf, R. (2001). The effectiveness of a group discrete trial instructional approach for preschoolers with developmental disabilities. *Research in Developmental Disabilities, 22*(3), 205-219.

Trousdale, A. M. (1990, February). Interactive storytelling: Scaffolding children's early narratives, *Language Arts, 67*(2), 164-173.

Turjillo, M. S. (2008). *Narrative development: Using questions to scaffold narrative production.* Retrieved November 18, 2009, from www.york.ac.uk/res/crl/esrc/PosterMacarenaSilva.pdf

Twachtman-Cullen, D. (1997). Comprehension: The power that fuels expression. *The Morning News*, 9-11.

References

Ukrainetz, T. A. (1998). Stickwriting stories: A quick and easy narrative notation strategy. *Language, Speech, and Hearing Services in the Schools, 29*, 197-207.

Ukrainetz, T. A. (2006). *Contextualized language intervention*. Eau Claire, WI: Thinking Publications.

Ukrainetz, T. A., & Gillam, R. B. (2009). The expressive elaboration of imaginative narratives by children with specific language impairment. *Journal of Speech, Language, and Hearing Research, 52*, 883-898.

van Kleeck, A., Vander Woude, J., & Hammett, L. (2006). Fostering literal and inferential language skills in head start preschoolers with language impairment using scripted book sharing discussions. *American Journal of Speech-Language Pathology, 15*(1), 1-11.

Vygotsky, L. S. (1978). *Mind in society: The development of higher psychological processes*. Cambridge, MA: Harvard University Press

Wellman, H. M., & Lui, D. (2004). Scaling of theory-of-mind tasks. *Child Development, 75*(2), 523-541.

Westby, C. E. (1985). Learning to talk talking to learn: Oral-literate language differences. In C. S. Simon (Ed.), *Communication skills and classroom success* (pp. 334-357). Eau Claire, WI: Thinking Publications.

Westby, C. E., & Wilson, D. (2005, November). *Children's play: The roots of language and literacy development*. Paper presented at the ASHA Convention, San Diego, CA.

Wiig, E. H., Secord, W. A., & Semel, E. (2004). *Clinical evaluation of language fundamentals – Preschool, second edition (CELF Preschool-2)*. Toronto, ONT: The Psychological Corporation/A Harcourt Assessment Company.

Whitehurst, G. J., Falco, F. L., Lonigan, C. J., Fischel, J. E., Debaryshe, B. D., Valdez-Menchaca, M. C., & Caulfield, M. (1988). Accelerating language development through picture book reading. *Developmental Psychology*, 552-559.

Wolfe, P., & Brandt, R. (1998). What do we know from brain research? *Educational Leadership, 56*(3), 8-13.

Wood, D., Bruner, J. S., & Ross, G. (1976). The role of tutoring and problem solving. *Journal of Child Psychology and Psychiatry, 17*, 89-100.

Yoder, P., Davis, B., & Bishop, K. (1994). Reciprocal sequential relations in conversations between parents and children with developmental delays. *Journal of Early Intervention, 18*, 362-379.

Zion, G. (1976). *Harry by the sea*. New York: HarperCollins.

Index

S

T